THE BOOK ON PUBLIC SPEAKING

Praises for

THE BOOK ON PUBLIC SPEAKING

"Topher Morrison is one of the most powerful professional speakers in America, and this book reveals how he's earned millions onstage, on camera and in business. I strongly recommend that you read it."

—**Steve Siebold**, CSP, past Chairman of The National Speaker's Association's Million Dollar Speakers Group.

"Effective presenting is one of the most important skills in business and, for that matter, life. In his book, Topher provides practical and effective strategies for becoming more comfortable with, and effective at, public speaking and business presentations. Whether you have one presentation to give, or have regular talks to deliver, read this book first."

—**Eric Edmeades**, Founder, WildFit

"I wake up every day thankful that Topher lives 4000 miles away! Topher Morrison is crazy good at training you how to communicate on-camera so that your business gets more attention. If he lived any closer, I'd have serious competition for my corporate clientele! But seriously, do what's in this book; your audience will thank you!"

—**James Lavers**, Professional Speaker, Founder, 'Selling from the Screen'

"I learned some amazing presentation techniques. I'm using them right now. They're awesome. You can't tell cause you're reading this."

—**John Heffron**, Winner of the Last Comic Standing

THE BOOK ON
PUBLIC
SPEAKING

TOPHER MORRISON

NEW YORK

NASHVILLE • MELBOURNE • VANCOUVER

THE BOOK ON PUBLIC SPEAKING

© 2017 **TOPHER MORRISON**

Published in New York, New York, by Morgan James Publishing. Morgan James and The Entrepreneurial Publisher are trademarks of Morgan James, LLC. www.MorganJamesPublishing.com

The Morgan James Speakers Group can bring authors to your live event. For more information or to book an event visit The Morgan James Speakers Group at www.TheMorganJamesSpeakersGroup.com.

ISBN 978-1-68350-321-7 paperback
ISBN 978-1-68350-351-4 eBook
Library of Congress Control Number: 2017900736

Cover Design by:
Chris Treccani
www.3dogdesign.net

Interior Design by:
Bonnie Bushman
The Whole Caboodle Graphic Design

In an effort to support local communities, raise awareness and funds, Morgan James Publishing donates a percentage of all book sales for the life of each book to Habitat for Humanity Peninsula and Greater Williamsburg.

Get involved today! Visit
www.MorganJamesBuilds.com

DEDICATION

This book is dedicated to the most powerful speaker I've ever known. She showed me that the most important trait a speaker can have is the ability to listen and love. The love she has, and her ability to listen to family, friends, and neighbors is unmatched. Thank you Mom, for inspiring me to be a better man. I love you.

TABLE OF CONTENTS

SPECIAL THANKS

To Jodi, for being my work wife, my alter ego, and the constant needle in my side to write this book.

To Sarah, my work mom. She's the youngest person in our company, and the most mature. She keeps Jodi and I on track more than we like to admit.

To Daniel, Glen, and Callum, you three make me the dumbest person in the room, and I love it!

To all of the people who have heckled me from the audience. Thanks for teaching me some powerful skills, but let's not make it a habit, okay?

To Zig for writing "See You At the Top," it's what pointed me in my life's direction.

To Ken for loaning me the book. Sorry, I lost it. I'll buy you a new one if you really need it.

To my brother Duane, if for no other reason than I don't want him saying, "Hey! What about me!?"

To my Mom and Dad for always encouraging me to pursue my crazy dreams.

FOREWORD

by Joel Comm

When asked what they are afraid of, people who responded to *The Chapman University Survey of American Fears* in 2015 provided dozens of answers. More than 30% of the respondents said they were either afraid of, or very afraid of, government corruption, terrorist attacks, credit card fraud, war, and reptiles. (Those darned alligators.) While some of the greatest fears were those that would lead to a person's ultimate demise, only 22% of respondents indicated they were afraid of dying. But there on the list, amongst those who are afraid of drones, loneliness, robots, volcanoes and floods, is the fear of public speaking. (Insert screeching violin sounds here!) "You mean you want me to stand up in front of a room of people and give a speech? I'd rather die!"

That might not be too far from the truth, as it turns out nearly 29% of respondents to this survey indicated they were afraid of public speaking. That's MORE people than are scared of perishing! I imagine that the very worst scenario for someone like this would be to actually die on stage from an alligator attack while speaking. The triple-whammy!

All kidding aside, I have a confession to make: I was a Speech Communications major at the University of Illinois in the 1980's. It wasn't because I wanted to become a better speaker. It was because I found myself in the liberal arts college and needed to choose *something*. History and Political Science weren't going to happen, so I chose the path of least resistance. Imagine my surprise when, in my junior year, I was told it was required to prepare and deliver speeches before my class.

Terrified.

That was the only word I could use to describe how I felt as the day approached. The only word I could use to convey how I felt the sleepless night before my talk. It's the only way I could possibly frame my twisted, wrenching insides as I held note cards in my hand and stumbled through my speech. Today, I speak to audiences of hundreds and thousands; and I love it. I don't get nervous any more. There are many reasons for this, experience not being the least among them. But there's one thing that I've realized in my career, and I remind myself each time I am preparing to take the stage, whether I am speaking to five or five thousand.

It's not about me.

The people in the audience are patiently waiting to hear what I have to say because the promoter of the event has confidence that I will be delivering value. They aren't there to watch me wrestle with my own anxieties. They are there to learn from me, to be inspired by me and/or to be entertained by me. My job is to put the focus on giving them my best. It's not about me.

And guess what? It's not about you, either!

It's about the value you bring to your audience through your passion, knowledge, talents, skills, ability, and unique personality. It's about how you have the opportunity to make a difference in someone's life. What a high privilege! And it's not one to be taken lightly. It's amazing how your fears can dissipate when you take your eyes off yourself and put them on those who came to glean from you.

Whether you are taking the stage or speaking to an audience through a camera, regardless of your fears, this book is designed to help you make the most of your speaking opportunity.

Topher Morrison knows a lot about public speaking, both from the actual speaking techniques and from the business angle. And *The Book on Public Speaking* is the most comprehensive guide I've discovered to be your ultimate reference guide on the business of public speaking.

Your audience has taken their seats.

The emcee is reading your bio.

He's just said your name!

Now, it's your turn to take the stage.

Go get 'em.

— **Joel Comm**, *New York Times* Best-Selling Author
& International Keynote Speaker

INTRODUCTION

I love watching light bulbs turn on. Not the ones over our heads, but the proverbial light bulbs inside. When I see someone in the audience 'light up' because of a connection they made with something important in their life to something I shared, it reaffirms I'm living my life's purpose—to contribute to the betterment of humankind.

My hope for this book is that it will not just make you a better speaker, but will give you the ability to construct your presentations in a way that people actually want to hear what you say. When that happens, you, too, will know the addictive bliss that comes when you witness someone in the audience 'light up.'

Since 1988 I've had the pleasure, honor, and responsibility of being a professional speaker. I've racked up nearly 2 million miles traveling the globe and I'm confident that there's not a situation that might happen on stage I haven't had to deal with.

This book can become your inoculation to some of the biggest speaker blunders I've seen, AND been guilty of committing. That's not to say you won't muck it up; you will—it's a part of being a speaker. All too often, I see people delivering a presentation they so desperately want to share with the world, but the world isn't listening. And it's not because the message isn't worth listening to—it is. But it's because the delivery of the message isn't presented in a way that works. This book will expose you to what works.

CHAPTER 1

ARE YOU THE NEXT GREAT SPEAKER?

E mbarrassingly, I have already accomplished every single thing in this book that I will advise you to avoid. And everything in this book I'm going to encourage you to do, I've stubbornly avoided at some point in my career. My writings in this book are from nearly 30 years' experience in the business as a professional speaker. **Learn from my mistakes and my wins.** If I had someone share with me what I'm about to share with you, it would have saved me ten times the frustration, and made me one thousand times the money one hundred times faster than I did over the span of my career.

I can't tell you how many business owners each month contact me asking for advice on public speaking. Some even wanting to get into the speaking business full time. While the names are different, the scenario is almost always the same.

"I want to inspire people to take their lives to the next level!"

"I want to help people live their life with passion."

"I want to help people tap into their full potential and start living the life of their dreams."

"I want to show people how to turn their dreams into reality"

"I feel my experiences could help out a lot of people."

The list goes on, and I can predict within remarkable accuracy who they are emulating. By the words they use, I can tell if they want to be like Tony Robbins, Zig Ziglar, Oprah Winfrey, or any of the other life-changing celebrated speakers in the market.

Here's the shocking truth. If you want to be the next Tony Robbins, Zig Ziglar, Gandhi, or Nelson Mandela, you will never become the next great one if all you do is reiterate the same lines from the people who inspire you.

If you want to be "the next great speaker," (and I mean this with absolute respect and admiration for the people I've mentioned above, and even those who I've left out) then stop setting your sights so low. **Think bigger. Think better. Be willing to say something people haven't heard before. Stop trying to be the NEXT anyone and instead, focus on being the FIRST of your own.** That's how those people I've mentioned above claimed their legacy. They delivered their knowledge in a fresh new way that nobody had ever heard before.

What Does It Take to be Great?

Being a great speaker in today's market goes beyond just getting on stage and making people laugh, or smile, or tear up from inspiration. There have never been more people vying for stage time—or trying to create the next viral video. If you really want to make an impact, you will want to focus on 3 main areas. And this book is broken down into 3 sections, each one reflecting one of these areas:

#1 On Stage—Developing the best stage persona you can. Trust me, just because you've been speaking your whole life, it doesn't qualify you to get on stage and speak. Make no mistake, that ease of dialogue and fluid conversation you see from the greats is all well-timed, rehearsed, and well-thought out. This book will show you the method to their madness.

#2 On Camera—Some of the world's best speakers on stage choke when they get in front of a camera. Or even worse, they try to use the same stage skills with a camera only to have mediocre results. This book will reveal specific techniques that work only for on-camera presentations so you'll be able to switch between your on-stage persona and on-camera persona for maximum effect to the viewer.

#3 Behind the Desk—This is actually the biggest part of being a great speaker. The amount of time you spend writing a speech, practicing a speech, and arranging the details of the negotiation for your appearance are all so critical, yet mostly overlooked with many of the speaker training programs you find in the market today. This section, in the end, will be your favorite part, because it will save you tens of thousands of dollars in mistakes, and will give you much more on the plus side when booking your appearances.

How Great Do You Really Need to Be?

There is a strange phenomenon in the speaking world. The overwhelming majority of speakers usually tell their audience the importance of always striving to improve in one form or another. The messages vary, but the underlying tone is all the same. And indeed, most speakers follow their own advice—in all areas except one: public speaking. They will become a student in every area of their life, but the one area that seems to get neglected is improving the way they communicate their messages. I'll assume you are one of the exceptions to this rule since you are reading a book right now on public speaking.

So why don't most speakers try to get better at their presentations? I believe there are two key reasons: #1. They've been speaking their whole life so how hard could it be? They think that it's just like speaking normally so it's no big deal. This makes about as much sense as thinking you can compete in the Olympics just because you've been running since you were a little child. #2. They've already received so much praise from people, they think they've already 'made it.' After all, why rock the boat? They have so many references for how great of a speaker they already are, why mess with such a proven track record of success?

This is why I'm sharing this insight with you, the exception to this way of thinking. I want to make sure you don't become one of the many who believe their praise. If you do, then you will plateau very early in your ability to move through the ranks of professional speaking. Yes, I realize I'm switching between the term public speaking and professional speaking. Keep reading; this will be covered in this chapter and it's a very important distinction.

Here's why being satisfied with your presentation skills creates a stagnant career. Audiences have varying degrees of approval, and even the worst speakers can find audiences that will approve. I feel it should be the goal of a professional speaker to hone their skills to the toughest of audiences—the ones that are the most difficult to impress. Once you can please them, you can wow any crowd.

What I'm about to tell you is going to ruffle some feathers. It's going to downright piss some readers off. If it angers you, then so be it. But if it does, I hope you will put the book down, vent, and then return to read this information as objectively as I'm writing it. I have no hidden agenda; I have no issue nor malice toward any of the groups

I'm about to identify. If you have spoken to any of these audiences and received praise from the group, I'm not taking anything away from your accomplishment. Rather, I'm trying to prevent you from falling flat on your face if/when you decide to progress to the next degree of audience approval.

There are certain people in the world who are natural skeptics. You might be one of them. Likewise, there are others who are, by default, more open-minded. You can satisfy an open-minded person far more easily than a skeptic. To impress a skeptic, you have to work much harder. You have to be more convincing, have evidence to back up your claims, and articulate your message far more powerfully with a skeptic than with someone who willingly accepts what you are saying because they are pre-disposed to possibilities.

Audiences are made up of people. Some audiences attract more open-minded people, others attract more skeptical people. It's important to realize something very important: whether an individual or a group is open-minded or skeptical, it doesn't determine how good they are as a person. This isn't a conversation about character, it's a conversation about how easily someone accepts what you tell them.

As a speaker, if you are sharing your thoughts with a group of open-minded people, they will be more likely to compliment you on your performance. It will feel great! They will line up just to have their picture taken with you to post on their Facebook wall. Speak to a group of skeptics and the room will clear out faster than a room full of kids who hear the ice cream truck driving by. And that's even if you deliver a technically flawless presentation!

So which type of audience do you want to speak to? My advice is to be that speaker who can get the biggest skeptics to sing your praise. Be the speaker who can get a room full of skeptical people to want to know more, want to get to know you more, and want to share with others how great your ideas are. And I recommend this not for ego, but for impact.

If you want to make the biggest impact possible, strive to be the best communicator you can.

The following is a list of audiences, as I see it, from the most open-minded, to the most skeptical.

- Faith-based Groups
- Multi-Level/Network Marketing Audiences
- Public, Self-Help Audiences
- Public, Business Development Audiences
- In-House, Company Training for Employees
- Leadership Training for C-Suite Executives
- Angel Investors
- Venture Capitalists

Again, this IS NOT a reflection of the quality of the audience. It's simply a matter of how easily impressed they are by a presentation. I've seen some amazing network marketing speakers who can bring the house down at a national direct marketing convention, and when they try to speak to a corporate leadership team, they are met with folded arms and a room full of suits checking their emails on their smartphones.

And I want to be clear: I'm not even remotely implying that spiritual leaders are bad speakers and couldn't impress a panel of investors. The fact is, there are many who can. They are amazing at what they do, and that's also why they are at the top of their game in their field. When you look at some of the greatest faith-based speakers like a Martin Luther King Jr., Billy Graham, or more recently, TD Jakes, Rick Warren, and the Dalai Lama, these speakers are clearly amazing, and could most likely win over the most skeptical people to their cause, and in some cases, have done so. Anthony Robbins, who has generated billions speaking to the public on self-help technologies, is so good at what he does that he can speak to any group of venture capitalists and most likely convince them to invest.

I also want to clarify that open-minded DOES NOT mean stupid—not by a long shot, so don't treat someone who is open-minded like they are stupid. If you do, they will not respond favorably. And I'm not for a moment saying that all churchgoers, network marketers, and lovers of self-help are open-minded either. I am saying that, by and large, when they gather into a large group, they are easier to persuade than a room full of skeptics. If you don't believe me, look at how many times the word "faith" and "believe" show up in a spiritually inspired message. Then count how many times "faith" and "believe" come up in a venture capital pitch for a multi-million dollar investment. Venture capitalists care less about what you believe or how much faith you have in your product, and are more focused on what you know for a fact and what the market has already proven.

So how great do you need to be as a speaker? It depends on how far up the scale you want to go from open-minded to skeptical. This book is written for the individual who wants to make an impact at any of those levels. I want you to be prepared for any audience you might face.

All Public Speakers are Broke

That's a pretty bold claim, and completely unsubstantiated. In fact, it's downright incorrect, because many public speakers have a day job that they rely on to make their money. But if a public speaker wants to earn a living being paid to speak, then they will need to transition from a *public speaker* to a *professional speaker*. What's the difference? Quite simply, a *public speaker* pays for the privilege to speak; a *professional speaker* gets the privilege of being paid for speaking.

At last count, the most popular public speaking organization is Toastmasters International, and in my opinion, it's the absolute best place to go to overcome your fear as a speaker and learn how to feel comfortable giving presentations. At my last check, they had nearly 250,000 members in more than 12,500 clubs in 106 countries, offering a proven and enjoyable way to practice public speaking.

The one thing missing, however, is a proven and enjoyable way to get paid for it. In fact, it's the opposite—you pay them to get up and practice speaking. Toastmasters is a great organization; they have helped hundreds of thousands of people correct bad habits like excessive "umms' and "uhhs" as well as fidgeting, and nervousness. They help you to work on your comedic timing, write speeches, and articulate your message more clearly. They aren't designed to teach you the business side of professional speaking.

This book is not only intended to share with you the most up-to-date skills for public speaking, it's also intended to help you become a professional speaker. Remember:

Public speakers pay for the privilege to speak.
Professional speakers get paid for the honor of speaking.

As a business owner, with the exception of philanthropy, it does you no good to be a public speaker. You're a professional, so I'm going to ask you to respect your value. This book is designed to set the record straight, and share with you some simple steps you can take, as well as alert you to some key errors you want to avoid when transitioning from *public* speaker to *professional* speaker.

Many entrepreneurs think they aren't a professional speaker because they first think of themselves as the person who runs their own non-speaking-related company. Make no mistake: if your ability to speak to the masses will end up in you garnering additional business for that company, regardless of what you think, you are a professional speaker. Embrace this, and present yourself as one.

For public speakers, those who are not paid to speak, the importance of speaking skill or business strategy leans in the direction of skill—about 85% to 15%. Focus your efforts on your ability to speak clearly, articulate your thoughts, and captivate your audience. This will make those times when you are on stage more enjoyable to you and your audience. It will be more emotionally rewarding and there's a good chance you will be asked to come back, or referred to other organizations to speak. This is also where most professional speakers start. It's where they 'cut their teeth' and learn the ins and outs of the art of mass-persuasion.

For professional speakers, those who are sought out and paid to speak, the importance of speaking skill or business strategy should lean in the direction of strategy—about 60% to 40%. Specifically in two main areas: sales and marketing. #1. Marketing your message to your target audience such that they feel compelled to call you over all the other speakers saying roughly the exact same thing that you are. #2. Selling your products/services. This includes selling your speech to potential promoters/audience members and then selling your products/services in the moment on stage.

Far too often, professional speakers spend 95% of their energy on strategy and 5% on their speaking skill. The result is a lot of speakers who are technically pretty poor speakers, but exceptional sales people and great manipulators. In my opinion, these are modern day snake-oil salesmen who ultimately only care about how much money they make on stage, and pay little attention to what happens to the audience member after they leave.

If you really want to become a professional speaker who is respected among your peers and promoters, has opportunities coming your way, and can sleep well at night knowing you have your audiences' best interest in mind as much as your own personal interests, then make sure you give as much attention to your speaking skills as well as your business strategies. Don't get lazy when learning how to communicate with power to the masses. The people who are taking time out of their busy lives, and in some cases, those who have parted with their hard-earned money deserve the best of you. You cannot give them your best if you do not demand the best from yourself.

If you want to be paid the kind of crazy speaking fees that professional speakers make, there is one thing that must happen for certain. You must gain credibility in the speaking profession. There are two ways to accelerate your credibility in this industry.

#1. Become a Specialist

Professional speaking is, in every way, a product that must be sold. Why should someone pay to hear you impart your message? You must be able to articulate your unique experiences and explain exactly how you can inspire others. If someone were to ask you right now what you speak on, what would you say? If your answer has anything to do with helping people tap into greater potential, find their passion, achieve peak performance, find their personal best, or achieve their goals, then you have A LOT of work to do. That is not a specialty.

A specialty has one promise that is simple, decisive, and clear. I have a keynote presentation about cooperating with your competition. Now you may be thinking, "But not everyone wants to hear about that." And you would be correct. That's the point. By specializing in this topic, I won't have people call me who aren't interested in that topic, but the ones who do will pay top dollar to hear me share with them exactly that message. If you would like to see a sample of the marketing for that keynote, you can visit this link: www.tophersbook.com/colkey

#2. Become a Published Author

There is something magical about becoming an author, both in the eyes of your customers and when looking in the mirror. I can't explain it, but speak with anyone who has made the painstakingly long journey toward having a book published and they will all agree. It transforms your certainty in yourself, and your credibility in the eyes of your customers. Before my first book, "Stop Chasing Perfection, and Settle for Excellence," I struggled to have anyone pay me more than $500 for a keynote presentation. Now my fees are $10,000. Would you like to know a secret? I still say the same message that I said when I was being paid $500 for a keynote. The difference came in the credibility.

Thanks to modern technology, you don't even need a big publisher to advance you hundreds of thousands of dollars to get a book deal. You can make a book deal with yourself today if you wish. In fact, you can have your book printed today if it's already written. There is a new technology that allows you to print books with as small of an order as— are you ready for this?—only one book! That's right, you can now print books one at a time. Although I have no affiliation, I'd like to share a link with you to help save some time and some money as you refine your speaking career. Check out this link and watch the video on the Espresso book machine; it's quite impressive.

http://www.ondemandbooks.com/home.htm

PART 1

ON STAGE

CHAPTER 2

HOW TO BEGIN A PRESENTATION

One of the biggest challenges you might have when crafting your presentation, especially if you haven't written a lot of speeches, is kicking it off in a dynamic way that grabs the audience and makes them want to sit up and listen. The techniques to accomplish this are varied. And for the most part, they all work, or at least at some point in history, they did work.

You've probably heard things from other speakers that you have to start off with an ice breaker—but if you aren't naturally funny, you could be setting yourself up for a dud right out of the gate. Just watch any Ted Cruz or Hillary Clinton political campaign speech when they try telling a joke, you'll see how devastating it can turn out. Even if you are quick with a joke and can get a good laugh, if your audience is a room of professionals or academics, it can still be rough waters because they aren't expecting humor. So unless it's so blatantly obvious it's a joke, they may wonder what it all means.

I had the opportunity to speak with a group of very powerful CEOs at 7:30 a.m. Most hadn't had their coffee yet, many were up late the night before and I started off by cracking a joke about the starting time of the event. I said, "For those of you who don't like starting off your conference at 7:30 am, that's what you get for electing Rhea as your chair. She thinks of 7:30 a.m. as 'first break'." Crickets.

Maybe you've heard that you should ask the audience an engaging question—but audiences are more sophisticated than they were back in the '80s and it will turn off a large percentage of the crowd. And when those questions become insultingly obvious like, "How many want to get the most out of today, can I see a show of hands?" or "How many want to make more money this year than you did last year?" the savvy audience member will immediately feel manipulated. This type of pandering to the audience works great for gullible crowds, but in the corporate world, the majority of people in the audience are savvy, well-educated, and even skeptical when listening.

You may have been given advice in the past to start off with a demonstration of some sort—but demonstrations can go wrong and in the world of professional speaking, if something can go wrong, it usually does. I'm quite certain whoever Murphy was, he was a professional speaker at some point in his life. If a demonstration requires any amount of dexterity, this can be a terrible way to begin. Those first few moments you are on stage are the most intense. Your adrenal glands will be wide open. Your heart rate will be up; and if that translates into shaky hands, your demo will instantly become way more difficult to perform on stage than it was a hundred times during practice.

Some people think you should get the audience up and dancing and shouting to raise their energy levels. This is a great technique if you are so boring you can't engage the audience, but most of the time, it just has a large percentage rolling their eyes and participating half-assed. But most speakers don't realize this because they are so focused on how great the dancing makes them feel that they fail to realize it's too much too soon for the average person in the conference room. I'm constantly challenged by this opinion by people who have attended an event by motivational speaking icon, Tony Robbins. He's famous for having loud music, smoke machines, and dancers on stage getting the crowd hyped. But there's a big difference between Tony Robbins and you on stage speaking to a crowd. #1. He has a reputation that precedes him, so he can pull it off much easier. #2. Typically, 40% of his audience has seen him speak before so they are pre-disposed to this activity and have prepared their newbie friends that they are bringing along. #3. Most importantly, even Tony doesn't begin his business events with dancing right from the beginning. He understands that he needs to earn the audiences' trust and respect before he gets them off their seats and jumping around. He understands the concept of 'right time, right place.'

So how should you begin a presentation? The answer is not intuitive, but once revealed it is slap-on-the-forehead obvious. You start your presentation off the same way the world's best stories begin.

Once Upon a Time...

These four words have been used since time immemorial to delight and entertain curious minds. It sets a stage that says, "We are about to go on an adventure." As a professional speaker, let your audience know that they are about to go on an emotional journey with you. Now you don't actually start your presentation off with the words, "Once upon a time…" For business leaders, that phrase is translated into a story that starts with a time and place different than where the audience currently is… and that time and place could be something as simple as five minutes before you went on stage when you were outside of the conference hall. Or it could be all the way back to when you were a child. Maybe before you were even born. Imagine sitting in the audience and hearing any of these three opening lines.

"Sixteen years ago I took a four-day vacation and instantly fell in love. When I met her I knew I was destined to be with her for the rest of my life. She was a city and her name was Tampa..."

"As I was preparing to walk up on stage to be with you today, no less than five minutes ago, a woman walked up to me and said, 'You seriously aren't going out on stage wearing those shoes are you?' Apparently she didn't like the fact that my shoes weren't polished. I told her, 'Don't worry, what I lack in shine for my shoes, I make up for in a polished presentation.' "

"In 412 A.D. the epicureans made a bold claim. They said that everything we do in life is for the purpose of avoiding pain, or gaining pleasure."

Notice how your mind instantly transports to a different time and place... a time and place where all the distractions you have in your day-to-day life don't exist. The effect is instant presence with the speaker. Now that presence, of course, is based on the notion that the "Once upon a time..." is of interest to your audience. Clearly the story you begin with needs to be something meaningful and relevant to your audience, and if the story isn't, the lesson to the story had better be, and you want to get to that lesson as soon as you possibly can.

Hold On, Let Me Stall

Here's another quick tip to capture your audience with a "once upon a time." Don't start with a preamble; just start with the story. If you preamble, it creates an impression that this is going to be a long, drawn-out story. It's also a waste of precious time. Particularly in the opening of a presentation, you have to win the audience over immediately—anything that delays that goal needs to go. Here's an example of how preambles slow down winning the audience's attention, and creates the impression that you're going to be telling a very long story. I'll use the same three stories from above.

"In order for you to understand why I love the city of Tampa so much, I'll have to take you back to the beginning. Sixteen years ago I took a four-day vacation and instantly fell in love. When I met her I knew I was destined to be with her for the rest of my life. She was a city and her name was Tampa..."

"People can sometimes do the strangest of things. To illustrate this, let me take you back to about 10 minutes ago back stage. As I was preparing to walk up on stage to be with you today, no less than five minutes ago, a woman walked up to me and said, 'You seriously aren't going out on stage wearing those shoes are you?' Apparently she didn't like the fact that my shoes weren't polished. I told her, 'Don't worry, what I lack in shine for shoes I make up for in a polished presentation.' "

"To better explain why so many people behave the way they do, we have to go back to before psychology was even a defined science. It began back in 412 A.D. The epicureans made a bold claim. They said that everything we do in life is for the purpose of avoiding pain, or gaining pleasure."

Notice how these preambles stall your attention, possibly even give you reason to stop paying attention. **So remember, if you want to tell somebody something, don't tell them you want to tell them something. Just tell them something.**

CHAPTER 3

SETTING THE STAGE

Nobody likes hearing silence when they walk up on stage. It's awkward. As a speaker, you'll probably enjoy your experience much more if you are greeted with a round of encouraging applause. But if you leave the introduction up to the organizer of the event, especially if it's a corporate event, this is an all-too-familiar scenario...

"All right guys listen up, we've got a motivational speaker in today to whip you guys into shape. So pay attention okay because he's got a lot of good things to say. So anyway um... he's gonna talk for the next hour so put away your phones and stop reading your emails. Um... His name is Topher and um... anyway... um... Topher do you wanna come up now?"

Don't leave this to chance. Have an introduction pre-created that you send in advance so the organizers can rehearse and read through it to familiarize themselves with the script. In reality, they won't. They won't even download the file. So print one out yourself and bring it to them, place it in their hands and say, *"Here's my introduction, if you could read this before you bring me up, I'd be grateful; it will set the tone of the speech and make sure they anticipate what's about to happen."*

When you hand them the introduction, have the font as large as possible, such that your entire introduction takes up the page. The bigger the font, the easier it will be for them to read. I recommend 18 – 24 pt Arial font. This will make sure they don't misread something or avoid reading it altogether because their vanity prevents them from putting on their glasses.

Inside the introduction you want to include some very specific things:

- Your credentials—Top 3 that give you the most credibility.
- The main benefits the audience will receive by paying attention.
- Specific instructions for the audience to applaud when you walk up on stage.

I prefer to give the promoter a selection of introductions that they can choose from based upon the audience and how they feel most comfortable introducing me. For example, I have a more straight-laced intro for the stuffy corporate world, and then a more humorous intro for groups who are very comfortable with one another where reading a general introduction might feel too stilted. Here they are:

General Introduction:
Our keynote speaker for today is Topher Morrison. Some of you may be familiar with Topher because he is the author of the best-selling book, "Collaboration Economy," a book that is being hailed as the go-to handbook for navigating the new economy. He is also featured in two hit movies, "The Compass"

and "Riches"—movies that chronicle the positive and negative experiences one receives when following their dreams and pursuing wealth.

He has earned a reputation for being the motivational speaker for people who are tired of motivational speakers.

What I like most about Topher is that he is shockingly honest, and in today's economic climate, we don't need someone who gets up here and tell us what we *want* to hear, what we want is someone who can get up here and tell us what we *need* to hear.

He's here today to share with us how we can increase job stability through intrapreneurship, create more consistent sales, and according to Topher, he says he'll even share with us how we can change the tides of the economy to our favor, and that all begins with a mindset. Here to share with us what that mindset is, ladies and gentleman, please give a warm welcome to Topher Morrison.

Humorous Introduction:

When our organizational committee met to decide who our keynote speaker would be, we all agreed on three things: They had to be well-respected, have a proven track record for producing positive results, and speak from a place of authority. We began our search and realized that those kinds of people were really expensive, so we settled for someone who is mildly funny, has no criminal convictions, and is able to speak without excessive drooling. Our search ended when we found Topher Morrison; he met two out of those three criteria.

Topher is here today to share with us how we can increase job stability through intrapreneurship, benefit from the current economic climate, and according to Topher, he says he'll even show us how to make it look like we are working when we are just playing solitaire on our PCs.

Ladies and gentleman, please help me welcome to the stage the self-help guru for people who are tired of self-help gurus… Topher Morrison!

Having multiple intros isn't necessary, but having one most certainly is. Don't leave your introduction to chance. How they bring you up on stage can determine if you start the speech off smoothly and with momentum, or have to work extra hard earning their attention.

Approachability from Stage

Have you ever noticed that some speakers just seem to be easier to approach than others? I'm not referring to physical access, but to emotional access. Some speakers are closed off and even if you try to approach them, while willing to communicate, they still don't leave you feeling as comfortable or as welcomed as others. There are some quick and simple things you can do as a speaker that will make you more or less approachable. Which effect you want to produce is entirely up to your personality. For me, I think it's better to be open and approachable.

I used to work with a professional speaker many years ago who would have his projector screen placed on a table that was situated by the corner of the stage. The projector cable would drape from the projector to his laptop computer that was sitting on another table of equal size on the stage. In addition to the laptop computer on the table, he would have a pitcher of water, a box of tissues, his cell phone, and random papers strewn about. There would be a music stand holding his training manual that was placed directly in front of his chair so he could read his notes easily. The one comment I would hear over and over from participants was how he wasn't very approachable. They would ask me a question about him and I would respond, "Why don't you ask him directly?" and they would reply, "Because you're easier to talk to."

One of the reasons he was so unapproachable was because of the fortress he had built around himself. When you looked at him on stage, it appeared as though he was hiding behind a series of obstacles, and in many respects, he was. Maybe not intentionally, but the message being sent non-verbally was one of being closed off.

Now some speakers like to be closed off from their audience. There's a speaker in the UK who has a bodyguard with him during his seminars at all times. No matter what size the audience, how much they paid, or how important of an audience they may be, he always has his bodyguard nearby. Most people laugh at the absurdity behind his back, but in his eyes, it increases his level of prestige.

So, depending upon your personality, you may wish to be closed off to your public, or open and approachable. If you want to be closed off, the solution is simple. Place as many people and objects as possible between you and your audience, especially during the breaks. If that's your goal, you don't need to read any further in this chapter. The rest of this chapter is designed to assist you in creating an open environment where people feel comfortable approaching you.

Perception Becomes Reality

To start, let's look at the attire and grooming habits of a speaker. Facial hair in the speaking business is usually taboo. The reason for this is because non-verbally, facial hair sends a message that you are hiding something. But it DOES NOT mean that the person with facial hair is actually hiding anything.

Unfortunately, a lot of non-verbal communication books do not effectively differentiate between the message something sends, and the reality of the situation. You could be the most open-hearted, authentic individual in the world and have nothing to hide whatsoever, but if you have facial hair, you will have to work harder to communicate that message than someone who has none. In the image below just notice if you feel differently about this person when he has facial hair vs. clean shaved.

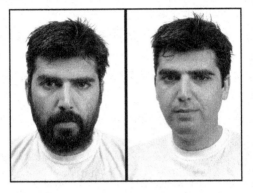

To See or Not to See, That isn't Really the Question

If your eyesight requires corrective lenses, be careful what type of glasses you wear on stage. As a professional speaker, it's best if you can wear frameless glasses. The thicker the frames, the thicker the barrier you've put between you and your audience. I'm not saying don't wear glasses. Being able to see your audience and any obstacles that might be on stage, generally speaking, is a good idea. Just be aware of what it looks like on the other side of the lens.

Hello, Is This Mic On?

There are many types of microphones you can use on stage. The type of microphone you choose to wear will also determine whether or not you are approachable or closed off. But with this decision comes some sacrifice. The best sounding microphones, especially if you are recording the event, are headsets. The challenge with headsets? They create yet another barrier. Personally, if I'm wearing a headset, I don't know if I should vogue like Madonna or grab my crotch like Michael Jackson, so I avoid them all together. I even have it as a rider in my contract that the venue must supply a lapel microphone. And they rarely honor it, so when I get there, I just wear the headset anyway. Remember, don't be a diva.

If you insist on wearing a headset, I would at the very least, encourage you to get an ear set instead. I have an ear set in cases where the venues don't have lapel mics available, and there is only one that I recommend. It's the most discreet and the preferred microphone for professional entertainers in musicals or plays where the microphones need to be invisible. The mic is made by Countryman. They are flesh-colored (they also have darker mics) and are virtually unseen. They wrap around the ear and hug the border of your jaw line, making them nearly invisible and the absolute best of what I still consider the worst-case scenario. To see these mics, visit: http://www.countryman.com/

At the time of this printing, my preferred microphone is a lapel mic. Until technology advances a bit more, it's going to remain my favorite. They clip on your lapel or tie and are unobtrusive. If you are wearing dark clothes, they are barely seen. Some of the newer lapel mics even mount underneath your shirt, making them completely invisible.

This leads to the compromise. Lapel mics are notorious for being hard to adjust the gains, which makes them prone to feedback. Headsets, on the other hand, are known for their great quality sound, and they never produce feedback. You can stand directly in front of a speaker and not hear any high-pitched squealing with a headset. If you are running your own sound system and it's a small venue with a small audience, feedback becomes a bigger issue. By wearing a lapel mic, you create the most open atmosphere, but that atmosphere may also be filled with irritation if you are deafening your audience with high pitched squeals. So take all these things into consideration when selecting your microphone.

The Stage

In addition to attire, the stage can be an invaluable asset to create a sense of openness and trust with the audience. Examine the two following diagrams. The individual is identical; the only thing different is the stage. Can you sense a difference? If polled, most people would agree that the individual in the second figure is far more approachable, and creates a more comfortable atmosphere.

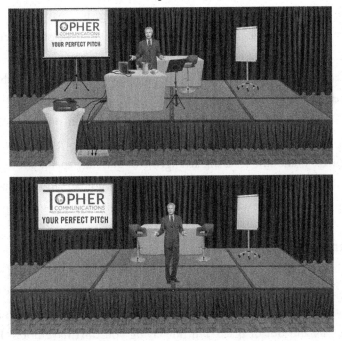

What are the secrets to create open and approachable energy? It's pretty simple, really. As mentioned previously, get as many things off stage as possible. Whatever is left on the stage should be as unobtrusive as possible. In addition, include some elements of nature, such as plants or flowers, which are appealing to the human eye.

Center Piece or Centered Peace?

Never underestimate the power of a floral arrangement on stage. It can immediately take a stale, corporate feel that traditionally is very cold and immediately warm the environment. When people receive flowers, it usually brings a smile to their face. These same psychological triggers are set off when we see a floral arrangement, regardless if it is for us or not. By having a floral arrangement on stage, it creates a subconscious feeling of receiving a gift.

Be careful to avoid flowers that are known allergens and ones that wilt easily. If the stage is lit with stage lighting, it usually gets pretty warm and the flowers can look pretty grim by the end of an evening, and especially by the end of a weekend event. This is why most speakers prefer a tropical arrangement. Tropical flowers can endure heat far better than daisies or carnations, and fewer people are allergic to them.

If you are going to be speaking in one location on a consistent basis, I recommend spending good money on a high quality artificial bouquet—make sure it's a silk arrangement. You may spend $300-$400 on an impressive arrangement, but it will never go bad, and after about four presentations, it will end up being far less expensive in the long run.

Dump the Music Stands

This is a pet peeve of mine. Musicians don't use lecterns to hold their music, so why should speakers use music stands to hold their notes? The notion of a music stand on stage for a professional speaker, to me, seems ridiculous and out of place. I'm not saying you can't have notes; I use notes all the time in my longer events. But I place them on a lectern. Here's why. Speakers trip over or knock over the music stand in almost every seminar I attend. These stands are flimsy and aren't designed to hold three-ring binders. The likelihood of your notes falling off is extremely high, and as a professional speaker, you want to do everything in your power to minimize mistakes. Lastly, if you have a music stand, it's too easy to just move it in front of you and that creates a barrier between you and your audience. Mainly, though, I think it just looks tacky to have a music stand on stage.

If you choose to use a lectern, have it off to the side as far as possible. I keep my lectern off the stage, and hidden behind my flip chart. This way, I still have access to the notes, but it's not blatantly obvious. If I need to consult my notes, I can walk to the flip chart and write something on the chart while taking a glimpse at my notes. In addition, for seminars I conduct close to home, I bring my own lectern made of Plexiglas (also known as Perspex in some countries). It is virtually unnoticeable.

Some Things Just Don't Compute

With the use of common PowerPoint presentations today, it's equally likely that you will see a laptop computer on the stage. While convenient, it's visually distracting and is yet another thing between you and your audience. This is where a lectern becomes quite valuable. You can store the notebook inside the lectern, making it invisible to the audience. There are several factors that will indicate whether I'm going to have the computer hidden in the lectern or off the stage completely.

If the seminar is flexible in content and I may need to add or subtract content based upon the speed at which the audience is getting the information, I may keep the computer on/near stage so I can quickly move to different sections in the slides.

Likewise, if I am less familiar with the content and don't have my slides memorized, I may keep the notebook on/near stage so I can visually see the next slide before it's displayed to the audience. Check the settings on your PowerPoint or Keynote software; you can adjust it so that the notebook computer displays the current screen the audience sees as well as the next slide for your personal reference. If you would like a quick video on how to do this, please visit www.tophersbook.com/ppsetup

If I have an A/V tech who knows my content well enough that they know what slide I should be on, I prefer to leave the computer off the stage and in their capable hands. This way I don't even need to mess with a remote clicker; they can do the transitions for me.

If I have the slides and content memorized so thoroughly that I never need to wonder what is about to approach and I know how the seminar will unfold each time, I prefer to leave the computer off stage. For example, I used to offer a weekend certification course. I conducted this seminar so many times I could literally set my watch anytime during the day based on the content I was teaching. Everything in the seminar was carefully choreographed and pre-planned. Even the jokes that seemed spontaneous were all completely mapped out in advance.

Screen Placement

It never ceases to amaze me when I go to a hotel venue to speak. I ask them if they have a projection screen and they proudly display a screen that lowers from the ceiling directly in the center of the stage. Whoever designed this clearly never consulted with a professional speaker about where they would like to have the screens. If they had, they would realize we want them off to the side. In a purely fact-driven, information, technology-based training program, perhaps the slide presentation would go best in the center of the screen, but for the majority of seminars out there, it's best off to the side. By having it on the side, you can place the projector off the stage and out of your line of sight with the audience, helping to reinforce openness once again. An even better solution is to have rear projection screens that allow you to take the projectors and put them back stage. While clearly the most professional, it does increase costs dramatically and may not be space-efficient.

Remember, the audience isn't coming to your seminar to see your slide presentation; they are coming to your seminar to see you! So make sure you are the featured object on the stage, not your slides.

If you haven't yet seen my SlideShare presentation on how to create effective PowerPoint slides, please check it out at www.tophersbook. com/greatslides

Ultimately, the fewer objects standing between you and your audience, the better. If you are a featured keynote at someone else's event, you may not have total control over all of these things I mentioned. For your own personal sanity, be flexible in all of the advice I've given you in this chapter and be okay knowing sometimes you'll show up to an event and they will have a huge table on the corner of the stage for your notebook computer, and pitcher of water, and products you are selling, and there may be a music stand (throw it away!). It's okay. At the end of the day, these are just helpful hints to improve your perception in the eyes of the audience. The biggest influencer in this will still be who you are as a person, how you interact personally with your audience, and whether you actually do care for them or not.

Memorizing Your Presentation

Around 11 p.m., I finally arrived at my venue. I was scheduled to speak the next morning to a group of entrepreneurs in Belgium. As I entered the facilities, I thought I'd made a mistake. This didn't look like a hotel. It looked like a mix between a public school and a jail. Concrete floors, brick walls, and dimly lit fluorescent lighting would take me to my 'hotel room.' The room wasn't any better, no art, no mini bar, no remote for the 19-inch TV mounted on the wall like a hospital room. Something was going to have to change for this speaking gig to be one I enjoyed. And the next day, it did. Big time.

I was going to share the day with another American speaker, Ron White—not the comedian Ron White, rather "The Human Phonebook" Ron White. And as long as we are on the topic of doling out distinctions, he was much more American than I was. Ron is a Texan. Not just a Texan—a retired military Texan (Thank you for your service in the Navy my friend).

I sat in the back of the room and watched a master at work. He was funny, he engaged the audience. He was the consummate professional speaker. He had the audience in the palm of his hand. They laughed at his jokes, and hung on his every word.

Earlier that morning he and I walked around the foyer to meet the other participants. He would shake their hand, get their name, ask them a quick question about their life, and move on to another person. When he got on stage, he would occasionally mention someone by name. "That's right, Bjorn, well done!" "Good point, Hilde!" "Thanks for asking that question, Myorka!" He didn't make a big deal out of it, but the audience sure did. They wanted to raise their hands and contribute just to see if he would mention them by name. And he did. Every single time! Not only that, but he continued his presentation flawlessly without ever having to look at his notes. (If you would like to learn how Ron did that, check out my interview with him by clicking here: www.tophersbook.com/ron

I was blown away by Ron, his perfect blend of professionalism and candor, and his ability to connect with every single person in that room—crummy hotel or not.

And you can do that, too. Every time you have to look away from the audience and consult your notes, you lose contact and break a connection. Memorizing a presentation is one of those things separating a novice from a professional.

CHAPTER 4

CRANK IT UP!

What Determines Your Rate

I am indebted to Steve Siebold, the heir to the Bill Gove legacy, for sharing with me what he learned from Bill, and what I am about to impart on you. There is one over-arching determinant that will predict how much money you make as a professional speaker, regardless whether you are getting paid an upfront speaking fee, from back-of-the-room sales, or from business generated for your company by speaking to a group.

To fully appreciate this distinction, let's start by examining the highest and the lowest paid professional speakers. I doubt anyone would argue that public school teachers are the lowest paid professional speakers on the planet. They work long hours, and are proportionately paid very little. Who are the highest paid professional speakers? This one always creates a bit of pause when I ask my audiences. Many think it's politicians. There's no question they are paid very well, but they don't even come close to being the highest paid. Some think that it's the motivational greats like Tony Robbins or Brian Tracy. Again, highly paid, but nowhere near the top. The highest paid professional speakers in the world are actors. Robert Downey Jr. has made $80 million to date for his role as Iron Man. Jennifer Lawrence made $52 million to date for her role as Katniss Everdeen in "The Hunger Games."

So teachers are the lowest paid, and actors are the highest paid. This is wrong. It's completely screwed up and should be reversed, quite frankly. But it is what it is, and there's nothing I could say in this book or from the stage that would change that. The change has to take place inside the system. School teachers need to tap into the indisputable truth about human nature, and only then will they be able to make a difference in their pay.

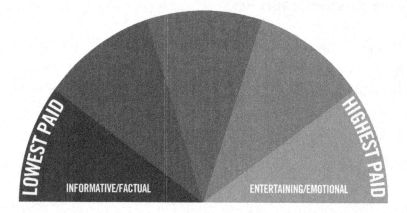

What Is That Truth?

Let's look at the facts: the lowest paid professional speakers spend the majority, if not all, of their time presenting content with very little entertainment value. The highest paid professional speakers spend the majority of their time, if not all of it, presenting something entertaining with little to no content.

The lowest paid speakers inform, the highest paid speakers entertain. That is the formula to becoming a highly-paid professional speaker. Think about it. As a professional speaker, we aren't stand-up comics, but we have to be funny. We aren't teachers, but we need to provide valuable content. We need to captivate an audience for sometimes hours on end, and we cannot do that just sharing content like a teacher. We must share that information in the most entertaining way possible. In the first two sections of this book, every strategy I share with you will be for the purpose of making you more entertaining, either in the front of the room, behind the mic, or in front of the camera.

If you are resisting the notion of being entertaining, because you feel that your information is more important, then replace the word entertaining with emoting. The real benefit from entertainment is that we feel a wide range of emotions. As a speaker, your goal is to emote to the audience and link those emotions to your content.

CHAPTER 5

BODY LANGUAGE

H ave you ever noticed how two speakers can say the exact same thing, but one turns you off while the other inspires you? Most of the time, the dynamism of a speaker has little to do with what they say or how they say it. It usually comes down to what they are saying with their body when they are speaking.

Virginia Satir—notably one of the most respected family therapists of all time—has compiled five postural themes of communication that, when understood and used with intention, can make or break a presentation.

It should be said that Virginia's work was not designed for speakers; it was used in family therapy to read the non-verbal indicators of patients to identify the themes or attitudes they were displaying when they were communicating. So while there isn't any official research on the effectiveness of using these postures as a speaker, I can tell you that from nearly 30 years' experience on stage, they absolutely make a difference in my delivery. If you want to learn more about these postures, they can be found in Virginia's book, "The New Peoplemaking." You can order it online by visiting: www.tophersbook.com/booklist

The Leveler

Out of the five postures identified in "The New Peoplemaking," this is the one that creates the most powerful level of sincerity and honesty. The Leveler is completely balanced and centered. This balance of posture sends a message of congruence to the observer. The legs are even, slightly narrower than shoulder width apart. The shoulders are level, and the hands are palms down Movement is purposeful and in harmony or rhythm with the speech.

This posture can create a feeling of believability with your audience. It can make them feel comfortable that what you are saying is the truth, and also increase their level of certainty with the notion that what you are saying is factual.

The Placater

This posture is a great pose to use to get you out of a tight spot. If you've overstepped your bounds or offended an audience, immediately move to the Placater position. This position is symmetrical, much like The Leveler, but with your arms outstretched and palms

facing up. Vary the length of your outstretched arms depending upon how apologetic you want to be.

This posture creates a feeling of sympathy and forgiveness. When you need to express a "don't shoot me, I'm just the messenger" attitude, the Placater is the way to go; but be careful, if used too much it can create a feeling that you don't know what you are talking about and are seeking their approval.

In general, you should use this posture sparingly and only with specific intention.

The Blamer

This posture conveys exactly what you might think—blame. The posture is leaning forward. One hand to the side, and the other moving outward and/or upward with the pointer finger extended. If you want

an audience to feel threatened, point directly at them, if you simply want to get their attention, point upward over their heads.

Use this posture sparingly because it can create a feeling of guilt or shame in your audience if you overuse it. There are some well-known speakers out there who use the blamer archetype so much that their audience feels abused by the end of the seminar. I remember seeing an American author speaking in London for the first time. He constantly used the Blamer position to communicate his points, but he misjudged the sensitivity of the audience and consequently turned off a great number of people.

The Computer

When you think of a computer, typically one thing is lacking: emotion. Computers are all about the raw data and facts. That's exactly what is conveyed when using the computer position. Shoulders are squared off much like in the leveler position, but this time, the arms are either folded, or one arm is across the waist and the other is moving diagonally toward the chin, most likely, with the hand holding the chin or face. In this position, there is a separation from the audience and the speaker. The arms serve as a sort of barrier and they cut off the emotional connection that an audience may feel toward a speaker. Use this position when you need to distance yourself from the audience, when you need to protect yourself from a verbal attack, or when you want to be more logical in your communication.

It helps the audience in moving out of their heart and into their head. If your audience is getting too tied into the emotional component of a story or when you want them to be in a more cerebral state, the computer is a great pose. Again, be careful not to use it too much or you will bore the audience and come across as uncaring.

The Distracter

Looking for a laugh? Then the Distracter is right for you! This is a fun posture that has little to no symmetry. It is purposefully asymmetrical and intentionally off balance. This posture is the exact opposite of the Leveler. When using the Leveler, you are conveying sincerity and honesty, with the Distracter, you don't want them to believe what you are saying, and it's used to inject levity in your communication.

This posture creates a feeling of light-heartedness and playfulness. When the audience needs a bit of a 'waking up' use a little Distracter with them. If you are making a statement that is intended to be funny but the words aren't blatantly humorous, this posture can be the difference. It's also a great posture to use after a joke bombs in order to get a delayed laugh.

Put it All Together

Used with intention, and choreographed into your presentation, these five postures can take you from being a ho-hum speaker to an outstanding speaker. Remember, when you are on stage, your present performance will dictate the demand for future bookings. Make sure you focus your attention on adding great value to your audience, while ensuring your performance is powerful enough that it compels them to want to see you again. This is how you get return bookings and develop a powerful reputation as a professional speaker.

If you would like to see these postures in action, please visit my YouTube channel at www.youtube.com/tophermorrisoninc and search for "Power Positions." Come back regularly, since I'm always posting new videos. In fact, take a look at all the videos of live presentations and see if you can identify where I'm using the postures mentioned in this chapter. And, why not take a moment to subscribe to my YouTube channel while you're there so you are updated the moment I upload a new video?

CHAPTER 6

HOW THICK IS YOUR SKIN?

So you think you are ready to be a professional speaker? Here's something the speaker training courses never tell you: You're going to be picked apart and scrutinized for your every behavior.

An old friend of mine and established speaker in the UK, David, was eating lunch before his seminar. One of his clients walked up to him and saw he was having a meal containing meat in it. She looked at Dave with a facial expression of judgment and disgust and said, "You're not a vegetarian? How can you teach spiritual practices and eat meat!?"

I have a YouTube video where I demonstrate working with a woman who had a balance disorder. Before we shot the video, she was unable to stand on one leg for even 15 seconds. After I worked with her, she was able to balance on one leg for over a minute. This is all on video. I had a viewer make the following comment. "Bullshit, I've suffered from a balance disorder my entire life, this guy is an asshole and I'd like to meet him so I could beat the crap out of him!" Normally, I would take a threat like that seriously, but in this case I figured if he ever did meet me and tried punching me, he'd probably just lose his balance and fall over anyway.

I've had people approach me during a break at seminars and tell me everything from how much of a jerk I am, to how I don't love people, to psychic predictions that warn me of doom and gloom in my life. Just recently I sent an email out to my customers asking for some feedback on the ad copy for a new product I'm coming out with. A woman responded that she didn't like my "1980's pimp outfit" in the video. Not exactly the kind of feedback I can apply since the videos are now all completely finished.

At one of my seminars where I train professional speakers, I had my girlfriend at the time and her two daughters with me at the ending celebration. I wanted everyone to gather round the table for a toast and some cake. My girlfriend declined and stayed in the background as silent support. She didn't want to steal any attention away from me, and wanted the toast to be something special between my customers and myself. After the toast, she then ate a piece of cake; I overheard two of the customers commenting how she obviously thought she was too good to eat and drink with us. Nothing could be further from the truth, but in the eyes of your customers, if anything can be misinterpreted, it probably will.

What's my point? In order to survive in this business you'd better make sure you have some pretty thick skin. As a professional speaker, you will be opening yourself, and your family members, to a life under the looking glass. Much like professional athletes and entertainers, the audience seems to think that because these people's jobs are in the public, it gives the viewers every right to make every part of their life public, and free reign to comment on anything without first considering feelings, or whether or not you even want to hear the feedback.

How will you endure the never-ending criticisms, the unsolicited blogs, and social media posts about you, your appearance, your philosophies on life, and everything else imaginable in between? Here's the best advice I can give you. It comes in three parts:

1) Separate Who You are as a Person from What You Are as a Product

When I say separate you as a person from what you are as a product, that's for you and your staff, not the public. The public won't have the capacity to do that. They will see your identity on stage as who you are in every facet of life. However, when you and your staff can separate these two very different aspects of yourself, it keeps you and them from taking offense, or letting a negative comment ruin the day. It also allows you to be able to hear the feedback from a place that might actually help you to improve.

At my Legacy course, we subjected our speakers-in-training to two weeks of feedback and actually assisted them in desensitizing themselves from harsh criticism so that they can remain calm and keep smiling when the public eventually goes on the attack or delivers well-meaning but ill-organized feedback for improvement. I would recommend you do the same as well. Make it your goal to get feedback every time you speak from a group you respect and trust. Don't let them say, "you did great, I can't think of any way you could improve." That's a copout and it's not going to help you improve. The only way you will improve is by getting direct and sometimes painful comments. I have a motto that says, "You never get better with 'good job'."

2) Be More Critical of Yourself than Anyone Else so Their Feedback Seems Lightweight

I'm all for having a positive mental attitude, and I'm not saying beat yourself up on your performances, but I am saying you should offer yourself the most specific and direct line of feedback that you can imagine. You don't have to share it with others if you don't want to, but do vocalize your feedback to yourself. Immediately after a seminar, I sit down with my staff and we take turns evaluating what worked, what didn't work, and what we missed. It's in these meetings that we have created some of our most valuable products and future sections for seminars. If you have a staff that you trust, and you invite them to be a part of this meeting, NEVER let them get away with just complimenting you and saying you did great. I know countless numbers of speakers who see these meetings as an opportunity for validation from their staff and their degree of closeness is directly proportionate to the degree by which the people compliment them and make them feel good. I'm colleagues with many famous speakers, but only close friends with just a few. Why? Because the majority of them don't appreciate anything other than a compliment. If you want to be a great speaker, don't settle for friends and colleagues that become "yes men." They'll never help you become better.

3) Don't Take Yourself Too Seriously

At the end of the day, I try to realize that I'm just another person on this blue marble who is just as big a dork as the next guy and I say equally stupid, if not more stupid things. Some of the ridiculous things that have come out of my mouth while on stage are truly laughable. It may not feel great at the time, but if you can laugh at yourself, and realize that you're always doing the best you can with the resources you have, then there is usually ample room for a good laugh or two.

You're Absolutely Right, Except for the Part Where You Talked!

Sometimes a customer's feedback is legitimate, other times it's way off base. The reality is, in their eyes, all of it is valid and they rarely, if ever, want to hear you justify why you can't incorporate their feedback immediately. So how should you respond? It's very simple. Commit this one sentence to your memory:

"Thank You for the Feedback."

Rehearse it over and over so it sounds sincere (ideally it's even better if you actually are sincere) and make sure you can say it with a smile on your face. Thanking them for feedback acknowledges that they have expressed their feelings to you. Remember, whether or not you agree with the feedback is irrelevant. In many cases they've spent a great deal of time and energy on constructing their thoughts and it takes courage to come up and speak with someone during a break. Acknowledge that thought, and their courage with a "thank you."

The reality is, you have so many things on your mind during a break the last thing you need floating around in your brain is some feedback that may or may not be valid, let alone feedback that hurts your feelings or brings up insecurities. So in addition to thanking them, you also should develop a strategy for getting the feedback out of your head and stored somewhere safe for evaluation after the event is over. Here's my tip:

After thanking them for the feedback, I give them the name of the event organizer in the back of the room. Ideally I point the person out and then ask them to immediately go share with that person the same things they shared with me so they can write it down and we can discuss it after the event is over. A reasonable person is usually more than happy to extend that courtesy and share it with the person who can actually do something about it.

CHAPTER 7

THE ART OF GIVING FEEDBACK

In the last chapter, we addressed strategies on how to receive feedback from your customers. In this chapter, we will address the most effective way to offer feedback, an equally important skill set every professional speaker must possess.

Depending upon the type of professional speaker you are, the feedback you offer will be different because your customer type will be completely different.

Seminar / Workshop Speakers

In a seminar environment, specifically workshops that have the participants incorporating the information being taught during exercises, it's quite common to have to offer feedback to an individual. Depending upon how this feedback is given, it can make or break the experience for the participant.

Generally speaking, feedback is best given immediately at the time you notice the need for the guidance. It does little to no good to approach one of your participants on the last day of the event and say, *"Do you remember that exercise we did on communication skills three days ago? I noticed during that exercise that you had some critical mistakes that could greatly impair your ability to succeed. May I offer you some feedback on that?"* That's about as effective as swatting your dog with a paper two weeks after it peed on your rug. It might make you feel better, but I doubt it's going to create any long-term improvements in your dog's behavior.

Immediate feedback, however, is not the best solution if the participant is in no space to receive it. This is why I prefer to open up any feedback dialogue with a question like, *"Are you in a space for some feedback?"* or *"May I offer some suggestions?"* Many speakers ask these types of questions, but deep down, they couldn't care less how the participant answers because they are going to give them the feedback regardless. I think this is a bad idea. I make sure that my participants feel safe saying "no." If they do say no, I simply respond with, "No worries. If we have time after the exercise, come see me, and if not, let's talk during the next break." It's better to give feedback to a participant in an open frame of mind an hour later than to give feedback in the moment to someone that is closed off.

Regardless of when you offer the feedback, I prefer to use the "Feedback Sandwich" method. **The feedback sandwich is some constructive criticism sandwiched in between two compliments.** In other words, I start off by complimenting them on something they did right, and then I offer the feedback for improvement, followed up with an overall positive statement. You will find that this methodology keeps the client receptive and in a positive state of mind.

The downside about that type of feedback is that some people only hear the 'bread' portion of the comments and don't hear the 'meat' of the feedback, which is where their need for improvement is located. In those cases, I give a sort of 'feedback pita pocket.' In other words, very little bread, and a lot of meat!

If you are concerned that they didn't hear the feedback or missed the point, then ask them to share with you what they will do differently in the future. It's a great way to confirm they received the feedback and interpreted it correctly.

Keynote Speakers

Rarely as a keynote speaker will you be giving feedback to individuals in the audience. Any feedback you offer will be to the event coordinator or the person who hired you. And it's important to realize that feedback should ONLY be offered if they have asked for it. Any unsolicited feedback, no matter how warranted it may be, will be interpreted as being arrogant and virtually guarantee you will never receive a follow-up call from them for future events. Even worse, you've killed a referral source, which for keynote speakers can add up to more than 40% of your future business (read on to learn how to make that happen).

Let's play a hypothetical game. You just finished your keynote speech. The event was poorly organized. They didn't send transport to pick you up at the airport and when you arrived at the hotel, they demanded a credit card even though it was supposed to be paid for by the company. To make matters worse, the time you were supposed to speak came and went and they had you go on at a completely different time, and at the end of your presentation, not so much as a 'thank you' was given by the organizer. Clearly, they could use your knowledge and expertise on how to create a more professional event in the future. Big problem: they haven't asked for any feedback on the event.

What do you do? Nothing—at least not yet. But the challenge with that is future bookings. You may want them to hire you again, because the money was great, but do you really want to endure all those hassles again? No, and you shouldn't have to. So what should you do? Wrap a time-release capsule around that feedback and save it for the future phone call. After every keynote presentation, I write a summary on what worked, what didn't, what I liked, and what drove me crazy. I keep it in my contact management software under the name of the organizer. If they ever call me back, I review the file and any improvement that I think they need to make is put in the contract. (i.e. "hotel accommodations including incidentals must be paid for by the organizing company" or "Transportation to and from the venue must be paid for and booked in advance by the event organization.") This way, it's simply a matter of clarification in the contract, not "hey you guys really messed up last time, fix it this time, okay?"

If the company that hired you does ask for your feedback (and they rarely do), then some tact and grace will go a long way. Follow the same process as mentioned above in *Seminar/Workshop Speakers*. Tell them what you really appreciated or liked, then offer the point of improvement followed up with an overall positive statement. If you do this, you will find that they are more than eager to make the improvement and you aren't seen as a pushy diva that is never satisfied.

It doesn't matter what type of customer you are working with if your feedback isn't received well, or if it offends the person receiving it. Remember this: the quality of your communication is equal to the response you get. Regroup, apologize for your poor way of communicating, and rephrase the feedback with a more appropriate response.

CHAPTER 8

HOW'S YOUR CREDIT?

I n the spring of 2010, I was waiting in the lobby of the San Diego Hard Rock hotel. Two of my friends from the UK, Dan and Nick, were attending a seminar at the hotel and we were going to catch up over dinner. As I stood in the lobby watching all the sexy San Diegans vying for attention as they showed off their latest overly priced designer brand clothes, I saw my old boss, Roger, from nearly 20 years ago speaking with hotel staff at the concierge desk. He recognized me instantly and we started to catch up on the years, knowing we only had a few moments before my buddies would arrive.

As two old colleagues do, we reminisced about our funny memories and pondered about whatever happened to "so-and-so" and "what's-his-name." During the conversation, he shared with me how one of the "so-and-so's" had threatened to sue him if he were to teach a seminar in the UK. The irony was that the person threatening to sue him was referring to intellectual property that he never owned in the first place and is commonly taught by many other speakers throughout the world already. In fact, the guy threatening to sue my old friend had made his living by repackaging all of the information he had learned 30 years ago from his mentors, but somehow over the years he had actually convinced himself the words he was saying were his own and he was the creator of everything he taught. But Roger and I knew nothing could be further from the truth. As we laughed about the absurdity, he shared a phrase with me that summed up the majority of speakers on the speaking circuit who delude themselves into thinking what they are saying is original, and lack the respect to roll credits to the people who originally inspired them. He said that a lot of speakers have a policy for giving credit where credit is due.

The first time they repeat something they picked up from someone else they say,

"As my good friend Bob said, ..."

The second time they repeat the pearl of wisdom they say,

"As a friend of mine once said, ..."

And the third time they steal the pearl of wisdom they say,

"As I've always said..."

I laughed so hard I was glad I didn't just drink a glass of water. That three-part phrase summed up so eloquently how people in this business can justify getting up on stage and teaching other people's content with no moral qualms whatsoever. And especially for beginning speakers, the ability to do this is far too tempting, and every speaker including myself has fallen guilty of such theft. But there will come a time in your profession where you begin to realize what it means to truly be a professional speaker. Professional speaking isn't just defined by your ability to wow an audience with "your" pearls of wisdom. It's about honoring the craft and taking pride in finding your original message. It's about realizing just how small the speaking circuit is and that when you steal the intellectual property of someone else, they will hear about it.

It's one thing to be respected by your audience, but one of the most rewarding things that can happen to you as a professional speaker is to be respected by your peers. And that will never come to fruition if you go down the path of becoming what is referred to in the business as a "speaker hack."

There are three reasons why I'm so passionate about encouraging speakers to find their own message. First, because I've felt the embarrassment of stealing other people's intellectual property first hand and it's humiliating. (See chapter 24—Protecting your Intellectual Property Rights) Second, because I've felt the financial impact of other speakers stealing mine. And third, because of a man named Tad James.

Dr. Tad James was one of my original teachers many, many moons ago. In fact, for nearly 10 years of my life I worked for his organization and travelled the world teaching on his behalf. It was an honor the entire time. Now Tad and I rarely agreed on anything, and I was always vocal about my disagreements, which I'm sure, must have been annoying for him. But no matter how many times we butted philosophical heads, I can honestly say with hand to my heart that he instilled within me one of the best habits a speaker could possess. Tad is adamant in his ability to cite his sources. I doubt I've ever heard him quote another without rolling the credits about where he got the information. It made a huge impact on me at the time, and I've always respected him immensely for that.

I believe that a lot of speakers subconsciously think that if they are quoting others and citing sources, their audience won't respect them or think of them as knowledgeable. The reality is just the opposite. **The more you cite your sources, the more your message has power. Citing your sources gives you credibility, and also gives your audience** additional places to seek information. But most of all, it's just the right thing to do.

How to Avoid Living in a Van Down by the River

What was once a respectable profession has become a joke. The world of professional speaking has been overrun by hacks simply echoing their favorite bits and bobs from the motivational speakers before them who left them inspired to become more. But like cover bands who try to sound exactly like the original, there's usually something missing. They sing the same words; they play the same notes. It's performed at the same tempo using the same instruments, but no matter how much they try to sound like the original, it just leaves the listener missing the original. The only time a cover band has you forget about missing the original artist is when they innovate the song beyond original recognition. When they put their individual spin on a classic, it instantly has a different effect. And in many cases, that effect leaves you liking the song even more.

If you're going to be covering material you've heard from someone else, then you'd better put your own spin on the piece. Be willing to add things that weren't in the original. Slow it down; speed it up; do anything except try to sound like the original. In fact, become the speaker equivalent of David Draiman from the band Disturbed. In 2016 they released a remake of Simon & Garfunkel's, "The Sound of Silence" and it became an instant viral sensation. The video has been viewed more than 75 million times at the publication of this book. It is so 'original' in every way—from the vocals, to the appearance of David, and the entire video production directed by Matt Mahurin—the whole experience is amazing. When you listen to the song, or watch the video, you don't miss Simon & Garfunkel. You are mesmerized by the updated song's 'originality'. Become your own speaking version of David Draiman. Check out the video here: www.tophersbook.com/draiman

Think about what was innovative and cool for music in the '70s. If you duplicate those sounds now, they can so easily sound like a joke. What once sounded cool now sounds corny.

Think about fashion in the '80s. If you dress today like you did then, people will think you are a fashion nightmare or going to an ironic '80s party. What once looked trendy looks like a costume now.

Think about architecture. If you design a building today that looks similar to a building designed in the '60s, it will immediately turn off the majority of prospective buyers. What once was state-of-the-art now looks antiquated.

I could keep going. The same can be said for electronics, automobiles, interior design, movies, and every other social or cultural trend. So is it so hard to believe that if you say things like the original speakers you may have heard 20 years ago, you will sound like a cliché?

When I use the word cliché, it may anger you. You may resist. You most likely will remember the impact they made on your life when you heard a speaker do or say these things, and you'll think there's no way that doing or saying these things now would bring any other effect than the same sense of wonder and awe they created for you. And if you continue to do them, you will be the speaker equivalent of that guy who still insists on wearing his Member's Only jacket today. Don't be that guy. This chapter is to serve as a warning. Avoid these clichés at all possible costs. They won't help you, they will simply annoy the sophisticated audiences, have them laugh at you in the all the wrong ways, and in some cases, lump you into a category of douchebag motivational speakers trying to manipulate the audience into becoming lemmings so they buy their products without using common sense.

Some of these clichés show up as slides, others might be how you behave, what you say, or the print you use to market your presentation. The way they surface varies. The effect they produce is almost always the same.

The Insultingly Obvious Questions

I was driving down to Sarasota to participate in a speakers meet-up with 20 other professionals, all using speaking in their careers in one way or another. The group was sophisticated. They were all people that I respect. I didn't want to deliver a lame presentation—I wanted to knock their socks off. So I practiced my five-minute presentation repeatedly on the 45-minute drive. When I got there, I was prepared. I was ready to leave them in awe. As I sat and watched each speaker present, I knew I was surrounded by pros. It was my time, I stood in front of the group and I was intimidated. But I was prepared. I gave my five- minute presentation and it was amazing.

"By a show of hands, how many here have someone in your life that you would do anything for? You know, that kind of person that if they called you in the middle of the night and said, 'I need you' you would get out of bed, get in your car, and go to them? They are that kind of person that if you were at work, and they called saying, 'it's an emergency,' you would leave work, lose pay if need be, and go to be with them because they mean that much to you. Not everybody can say yes to that question, but by a show of hands, how many are fortunate in life to have someone that you love that much? [Wait for response]. Great, now let me ask you another question. Wouldn't it be great if that someone you were just thinking of was yourself? You know, I've been asking that question to audiences all over the world for the past 10 years and in every single instance, not one person was ever thinking of themselves. I'll know I've done my job here today when I ask that question and the first person you think of is yourself."

I'd delivered this vignette well over 500 times throughout my career. When I got done, I was ready to hear the audience carry on about how great it was and be stumped for how I could make it any better. Much to my humility, they all had something to say about how to make it better. But one guy's feedback hit me in the gut. It angered me. I resented him, and it wasn't until my drive home that I was able to calm down, actually hear what he said, and discover how right he was.

During the presentation I asked the audience a question. I asked them to raise their hands if they could relate to what I was talking about. During his feedback he said these painful words: "Don't ask me a question that you don't care about the answer to. It's insulting to me and everyone in the audience." How could he assume I didn't care about the answer? That's one of the things that makes me different from so many other speakers that I can't stand. I ACTUALLY CARE ABOUT MY AUDIENCE!!! He was a jerk and he obviously didn't understand where I was coming from. But once I calmed down, I remembered one of my principle beliefs in life that I use to improve.

Advice Only Works if You Use it

So I had a choice. I could use his advice, or dismiss it. So I asked a very painful question. What if I really didn't care about the answer from my audience? And as I asked that question, what came up was very hard to swallow. I didn't care about the answer. I didn't actually care whether they raised their hand or not. And I knew I didn't care because whether they raised their hand or not, I was going to say the exact same thing. And it led me to realize how often speakers ask what I now refer to as the insultingly obvious question.

I'm not saying all questions are insultingly obvious. I still ask my audiences questions, and in some cases, I may even ask them to raise their hands (I will avoid that if at all possible). But when I do, I have an outcome. I need the data. And I will alter my course in the presentation based upon the answers I get from the crowd. Not all questions are insultingly obvious. So how do you know which ones you ask are irrelevant vs. insultingly obvious? If you are going to say the same thing regardless if they answer yes or no, raise their hand or don't, then it is probably an insultingly obvious question, and you don't need to ask it.

What should you do instead? Answer the question for them, and even tell them you won't insult their intelligence by asking a stupid question.

For Example:

"I'll bet if I were to ask everyone here if you have someone in your life that you would do anything for, the majority of you would probably raise your hand. I'm not going to ask you that question, but if I did, I'm sure the majority can think of someone. You know, it's that kind of person that if they called you in the middle of the night and said, 'I need you,' you would get out of bed, get in your car, and go to them. They are that kind of person that if you were at work, and they called saying, 'it's an emergency,' you would leave work, lose pay if need be, and go to be with them because they mean that much to you. And as you think about that person right now, wouldn't it be great if that someone you were just thinking of was yourself? Now if you were actually thinking of yourself, congratulations, but I've been asking that question to audiences all over the world for the past 10 years and in every single instance, not one person was ever thinking of themselves. So I'll know I've done my job here today, if, when I ask you to think of that special someone you would do anything for, that the first person you think of is yourself."

I was able to produce the exact same effect in the second example as the first, but I did so without having to ask people to raise their hands. I didn't have to ask insultingly obvious questions, and even more importantly, nobody had to feel embarrassed publicly if they couldn't think of someone and didn't raise their hands. Same effect, much more sophisticated. From now on, just answer the question for them and you'll be much more appreciated by your audience.

Can I Not Have This Dance?

Since the explosion of motivational seminars in the '80s there has been one undisputed king of events—Tony Robbins. His events have inspired thousands of people to enter the field of motivational speaking. He has a way of getting some of the most resistant people in his audience to jump up and down, follow the dancers on stage, and "whoa clap" all night long. Many would-be speakers remember how great it felt that first time they felt unchained from ego and danced like a fool to Tony's signature song, Jock Jams', "Are You Ready for This?" That feeling was so intense as they entered the professional speaking world they couldn't wait to jam the music, get their audience in a frenzy, and rekindle those emotions. Nearly all of them have failed this goal miserably.

Why? They didn't take the time to learn the true craft of professional speaking. Instead, stitched together their favorite bits and bobs from all their favorite speakers in some sort of strange "best of motivational hits," thinking that if they just combined all the best bits with the best bobs, they will have an even more amazing seminar. These speakers failed to realize a critical component. The reason why their favorite bits and bobs of an event were so powerful was because of the 20- or 30-minute setup before they got to it. Unwittingly, they just took the favorite part without including the most critical steps leading up to it. The result is a weird knock-off that never produces a similar result. No better example of this is the speaker who gets on stage and forces their audience into some sort of awkward "dance off" that is about as silly as Breakin' 2— Electric Boogaloo. (Google it) The justification that many speakers use for these antics is that it keeps the audience engaged and entertained, and if done correctly, it can, but so many people are doing it incorrectly, that it's just become cliché.

So what should you do instead? Be so entertaining as a speaker that your audience genuinely enjoys listening to you. How can you be that entertaining? You follow the format for entertainment that has been in existence since the art of storytelling has come alive. This three-part formula has best been described by the famous mythologist Joseph Campbell, and any good storyteller should study his work. But in the age of our attention span being limited to tweets 140 characters or less, perhaps the best person to simplify this whole process was the legendary professional speaker, Bill Gove. His theory for a good story?

Part 1—Start with a Premise
Part 2—Create a Problem
Part 3—Find a Solution

Audience members shouldn't have to work to figure out what the premise of the story is all about. If you convolute your story with subplots, irrelevant side comments, and unnecessary dialogue that doesn't contribute to the value of the story, it's just going to leave the listener confused and wanting to check out. For example: Premise—Boy meets girl. Problem—Boy loses girl. Solution—Boy wins girl back.

Hey! Look at my Ferrari!!!

Avoid putting photos of you in your slide presentations standing in front of your Ferrari, yacht, or mansion. Leave out the pictures of you standing next to Richard Branson or Elon Musk. Let's be honest, you probably just asked them for the photo and they agreed so you would leave them alone a bit faster. (Full confession: that's what I did when I met Richard Branson.) It's misleading to the audience to imply you are best buddies. And even if you are, they probably don't appreciate you using their status for you to bump up your credibility. You might think this helps the audience respect you or look up to you. It doesn't. At least not the sophisticated audience. The only people this will impress are gullible people looking for a savior.

You might argue that it's not about credibility, it's about inspiration. You want to inspire the audience to set goals to own their own Ferrari, sail around the world on their own yacht, or retire in their own massive mansion. It's a worthy and respectable ambition, but when an audience member is looking at a picture of you standing in front of your Ferrari, there's no room in the picture for them to imagine themselves in the picture.

So what should you do instead? First off, take yourself out of the picture—because it's not about you! And I don't just mean take a picture of your exotic car or home without you in the picture and say, "Hey look at my mansion, you can own one, too!" I mean take you AND your toys out of the picture. Get rid of the slide all together and replace it with a dialogue that compels the listener to create their own pictures in their mind that are far more motivating, enticing, and personal to them than you pushing your goals on them could ever be. So your presentation might transform from,

"Here's a picture of me standing in front of all my exotic cars parked out front of my million-dollar mansion, isn't that cool? If you do the three things I'm going to share with you today, you, too can have your very own Ferrari and mansion in Beverly Hills!"

Into something truly inspiring like,

"I have three strategies to share with you today that have worked very well in my life. And it's my hope that you walk away today and use these strategies to produce something even better for you. Do you remember that exotic car you dreamt of owning as a child? Did you ever drive by a beautiful home and wonder what it would be like to live in such a place? These luxuries are within your reach. It starts by vividly imagining yourself in that special car. See yourself sitting in that dream home. Can you do that now? Because the first piece is going there in your mind. The second piece is doing three things in your world right now that make your imagination come to life. That's what today is about—discovering AND actually doing these three things that I've already field tested for you. I know they work. They did for me, and they will for you..."

I Already Know About You

Similar to the vanity pictures of you standing in front of your exotic car is the slide that often accompanies the phrase, "Before I go into my presentation, here's a little bit about me." No one cares about you. They really don't. They care about themselves. They want to know how your knowledge that you are going to share with them this day is going to make the rest of their days better. And hearing about your life's story in five minutes or less doesn't add value; it postpones value. You might argue that you need to talk about your accomplishments in order to gain credibility with the crowd. Valid point. Credibility is something very important. Your audience should see you as an expert in your topic, and have faith that what you are about to share will produce similar results in their life. But you talking about yourself rarely makes this happen.

What should you do instead? **Have a powerful introduction that sets the tone for your appearance.** Whoever introduces you to the front of the stage is the person who should be bragging about your list of accomplishments. You don't need to repeat them. Remember when *someone else* talks about how accomplished you are, the audience will be impressed. If you talk about how accomplished you are, people will most likely be turned off and bored.

You Didn't Kill Yourself

We've all had low points in our lives. For some, maybe you, it was really low. So low you wanted to check out. It might surprise you that the majority of the people in this world, at one point or another, were in so much pain that they contemplated or wished they could just fall asleep and not wake up. But wishing you were dead is a far cry from actually attempting suicide that left you in the hospital. Don't dramatize your low points to where you tell your audience, "All I wanted to do was die." Because after you've delivered that presentation enough times, it will evolve to, "I actually contemplated suicide." And then, eventually it will become, "At one point, I even tried killing myself." Stop it. No you didn't. If you don't have the scars or hospital bill to prove it, you really didn't try killing yourself. At best, you tried getting attention from someone. So don't disrespect those few who have actually tried taking their own life by turning your pain into a 'fiction-based-in-fact' fantasy.

What if you actually do have the scars or hospital bill to prove it? Congratulations, you've pulled through a very difficult time in your life and you should be proud of that accomplishment. But you shouldn't brag about it to strangers either. And there are several reasons why.

#1. The majority of the people in the audience won't be inspired— they will be judgmental. They might even see you as a weak-minded individual who can't handle the challenges of life. They have no right to judge you so unfairly, but they will. Why place an obstacle in your presentation that you now have to overcome? It's best to eliminate self-incriminating stories that make it harder for you to gain the respect of your crowd.

#2. For the small percentage (and it really is an incredibly small percentage) of the people in the audience who are contemplating suicide, your story most likely won't help them anyway. Why? Because when someone is on the verge of suicide, they typically have a sense that no matter how tough you or anyone else had it, it still can't be as tough as how they have it now. Don't try comparing your life's past to someone else's current situation. It won't compare in their minds.

#3. There are so many people on the speaking circuit using their (usually over-exaggerated) story of attempted suicide that they've watered down the emotional impact of your very real-life encounter with attempted suicide. It's not fair, but it is the way it is. So find a better way to inspire your audience—this angle is no longer innovative or effective, and, in fact, can be dangerous and disheartening.

Next!?

Don't describe yourself as the next Tony Robbins—or Les Brown—or Oprah Winfrey. Don't tell people your company or product is the next anything either. If you look at the most innovative brands on the market today, you can almost guarantee that there is someone out their claiming to be the "next" or "new" version of it. At the time this book was published everyone was trying to be "The next Uber." Before that, software developers were competing to be "The next Facebook." Go back even further and companies were boasting about being "The New Coke." And in that bizarre case it was actually the old Coke trying to outdo itself. #Fail. Interestingly, those who were claiming to be the "next" or "best" never became as successful as the companies they were trying to one up.

So what should you do instead? Be the first and only you. The most innovative companies like Facebook never claimed to be "The next MySpace." Apple never bragged about the iPod being "The next Walkman." Netflix didn't say, "We are the new Blockbuster." Innovative companies don't want to be the next anything. They want to be the best of the first for what they do. And as a professional speaker, you don't want to be the next person others already have heard of, you want to be the first person who has ever said something the way you say it.

Don't Be L.A.M.E.

Acronyms were kind of cool back in the day, but then again, so was smoking, polyester leisure suits, and the dating game with Chuck Woolery. But we've moved beyond them. We are more sophisticated and let's be honest; how many more acronyms do we really need for S.U.C.C.E.S.S.?

And in nearly every case where a speaker is using an acronym, they usually have one letter that just doesn't make sense and you can feel the desperation in them trying to force the acronym into making sense.

"And S stands for So happy to be alive!" Really? I'm pretty sure that should be H for Happy, but since the word didn't have an H in it, they just forced something non-related into it.

If you think it helps the audience remember your key points, you're wrong. They probably won't even remember the word. In fact, just like the speaker usually has to force one abbreviation in a word to conform to what they are really trying to say, in almost every situation, someone stops paying attention, and as you are finishing up the acronym someone raises their hand and shouts, "I'm sorry, what did the S stand for?"

Save us the agony… just tell us what you want us to know; don't try to make it fit into an acronym. (Full confession, in my first book, "Stop Chasing Perfection, and Settle for Excellence," you will find a chapter with acronyms. I also had a Flock of Seagulls haircut in high school. We evolve.)

Now if you are hell-bent on using acronyms, fine. But if you must, at least use words that aren't overused like S.U.C.C.E.S.S., G.O.A.L.S., and L.E.A.D.E.R.S.H.I.P. My friend Alex Rodriguez uses B.A.C.O.N. as an acronym for his strategy to launch products in the book, "Digital Bacon." He's probably the only person who has an acronym for the word "bacon." And even if he isn't, it's still cool. Because, well… it's bacon!

What Level is This?

Stop telling people you want to help them get "to the next level." That phrase represents the most overused four words in the professional speaking world. "I want to help you take your career to the next level!" "Let's take your relationship to the next level!" "I want you to take your motivation to the next level!" "It's time to take your fitness to the next level!" Just stop it. And while we are at it, avoid other unquantifiable phrases like, "tap into your true potential," "live the life you deserve," or "Live your authentic life." All of these phrases sound amazing and still might have an effect on a gullible crowd, but there are several problems when you use such generic terms, no matter what audience you are speaking to.

Instead, try being specific. Really specific. When you are direct and specific in your communication, you have a better chance of helping someone achieve their goals, because you know whether or not their goals are actually achievable. If you tell someone, "I can help you take your career to the next level" and for them, "the next level" is to become a billionaire by the time they are 30 (and they are 28) with no clear path on how to get there, you just set yourself and your client up for failure. At best, you've just made it a highly unlikely long-shot. If, however, you tell your audience you want to help them reduce their body fat by 5% in five weeks with just five simple exercises they can do in 15 minutes a day, that is far more specific and your advice in your presentation will be more likely to achieve that desired outcome.

There's another, far more important reason why, as a professional speaker, you want to use specific words—words that create imagery in the clients minds. The average human brain dedicates approximately 60% of its brain mass to the visual processes. If your words do not create images in your audience's mind, then you run the risk of putting the majority of their brain to sleep, and their mind will wander and they will stop listening. If I say, "I help speakers take their speaking career to the next level." There are no pictures in your mind. And even if you could argue that you are thinking of some pictures, the problem with that is that I don't know what pictures they are, so I'm not sure I can actually deliver what you are imagining that I can. But if I say, "I help professionals like yourself go home at the end of the day knowing that their calendar is filled with speaking engagements, and all their bills are paid with money left over in the bank. So when they go home they can be present and enjoy the company of the people they love without worry or stress about what's happening at the office." That is far more specific!

Take the time to really think about what you are promising with your words, and ask yourself what the specific outcome would be for someone if they did what you told them to do. Start with that description and you'll find your audience is far more receptive than if you had just said, "... to the next level." Now let's go on to the next chapter.

CHAPTER 9

HOW'S YOUR ENERGY?

This chapter could be one of the most important contributions to your success as a professional speaker. How you market yourself goes way beyond your website and brochures. In fact, the most important part of your marketing is how you will interact with people at your events. The challenge with that is every person you meet will behave differently toward you. Some will get right up in your face and have no awareness of your personal space, others will always want to keep a healthy distance, and if you move too close, they will just back away. How you choose to interact with either type of person will determine what they say about you long after you have parted ways. "He seemed distant and unapproachable; I felt like he didn't want me to talk to him." "She was a little too aggressive, she got right up in my face and wouldn't back off." These types of audience comments stem from a speaker who doesn't know how to gauge the personal space of others and act according. You might be thinking, "but what about my personal space?" While I empathize, it's irrelevant. When you choose to put yourself out in front of the masses, you must be there for them; not for you. Follow these simple visualizations and the comments people will say about you will be, "He was so easy to talk too! I felt like we really connected!"

The people who back away are much easier to work with. You just gauge their personal space and if you see them pulling back, you should back off yourself by just a few inches. The troublemakers are those people who need to get two inches in front of your face with no consideration for your personal space. How do you deal with these people? It's quite simple really, but in order to master this delicate balance, you need to become aware of both your energy and the people around you.

When I say energy, don't worry, I'm not going to tell you to get your chakras balanced, burn sage around your seminar room, or have Sylvia Browne do a reading on you. The energy I'm speaking of is that imaginary bubble around your body you most likely call your personal space. We all have it. We can't touch it or see it, but we can all feel it. If someone gets just an inch or two inside our personal space, we feel invaded. If they get too far away from our space, we lean in and subconsciously get closer to them so we can "feel connected" to them.

What most people don't realize is that this personal space can be changed. As a speaker, it has three distinct uses. The first is to feel more comfortable around those face-to-face people who seem like they are going to kiss you every time they engage in dialogue. The next is to ensure you don't encroach on other's space and have them feel like you are being invasive or 'too intense.' And lastly, you can use this to connect with an entire audience no matter the size. In fact, this technique is absolutely necessary when you speak with convention-

or stadium-sized audiences to keep even the back row engaged and connected with you.

First, take a moment to find your own personal space. This is probably easiest to do if you approach someone, preferably someone you don't know. Slowly move closer to them until you feel slightly uncomfortable, then back off by just an inch or so. Whatever the distance is between you and that person, that's probably your personal space. The challenge with doing this, of course, is you might get slapped when you just approach a total stranger without saying a word. So a perfectly acceptable alternative is to have a friend or co-worker (someone you aren't intimate with) as the test subject to practice your own personal space. Have them approach you slowly, and the moment you feel they are getting uncomfortably close, put your hand up. That is your own personal space.

I Don't Mean to Pop Your Bubble

Now, try this visualization process:

- Slowly imagine your personal space (or personal bubble) around you moving closer toward you. Inch by inch, just imagine that space getting closer and closer to you.
- Once you've pulled that bubble so close it's only a few inches away from your body and face, have your friend approach again and notice how much closer they can get to you without feeling uncomfortable. Remember, if they haven't done this visualization for themselves, they might feel uncomfortable, but

that's not the point of this exercise. The point is to make it easier for you to tolerate people at your events who seem to have little or no personal space of their own, and love to get face to face with anyone they come in contact with.

- Once you do this a few times, you'll discover you can pull this personal space in very quickly. It's an invaluable tool to make sure you don't back away from those people who really want to connect with you, and want to do that in a personal space that otherwise would be too close for comfort.

The second purpose is to make sure you don't encroach on someone else's personal space. To practice this:

- Slowly approach this same person but look closely at their non-verbal cues. The moment you get too close for comfort you will see some reaction from them, and it can sometimes be very subtle: their head slightly pulls back, their eyebrows raise, their head turns slightly to the side like an intimidated Chihuahua, their neck stiffens, their mouth smirks, and if you go even further they will actually step backward.

- Practice this until you can see the most subtle of changes in their physiology. When you can do this, you can accurately gauge someone else's personal space and be conscious not to invade it.

The third purpose of changing your personal bubble is to do just the opposite, and send your bubble of energy out so far when you are speaking to an audience that it encompasses the entire room. The world's best speakers realize this and purposefully make sure they send their energy all the way to the back wall of the room they are speaking in. This is why some speakers can engage an audience in an auditorium while others can't keep the attention of 10 people in a board room. It's all about energy. Where are you projecting it when you speak?

Try this exercise.

- Stand in a room full of people, maybe a cocktail party or bar after work. Stand anywhere in the room you wish, maybe even against a wall.
- Take that same bubble that you worked with previously, but instead of bringing it inward and close to you, send it outwardly and imagine this bubble of energy embracing everyone in the room.
- Imagine it reaching all the way to the opposite walls, and then slowly drawing back in as if hugging each person in the room drawing them toward you.
- If you do this correctly, you will most likely attract conversation toward you. People will approach you. They may even compliment you on your energy or say that you seem to light up the room. This may take a bit more practice than pulling the energy bubble close to you as described earlier, but with time and practice, you'll discover it's the determining difference from someone who lights up a room or becomes a wallflower.

As a speaker, you must learn how to control your energy, and project this out to the very back row. By doing this, your audience will stay more engaged and they will feel connected to you far better.

The more you work with your own personal energy or personal space, the easier it will be to make changes in interacting with delegates at a moment's notice before and after your program. The more effective you can become at expanding your energy to the back row of the audience, the more you'll notice the audience members maintaining attention and feeling connected.

CHAPTER 10

THE CONTROVERSIAL TRUTH ABOUT SELLING FROM THE STAGE

WARNING: I am not very polite in this chapter: Don't read if you are easily offended.

This brief chapter contains the secret to creating massive sales from the stage and creating a feeding frenzy of people rushing to the back of the room at your events. The technique I'm about to share with you works better than any other technique you would hear at any other speaker training program. Are you ready?

Hard close the shit out of your audience and constantly be selling throughout your speech.

That's it... and I'm going to prove to you why this is the best technique if you want to make the most amount of money possible.

The kind of speakers who follow this philosophy are nothing more than sleazy salespeople who only care about one thing: Making shit loads of money and making it as fast as they can. This is why they hard close like crazy and never provide any real value. Think about it. If there actually was a better way to sell from the stage, those sleazy salespeople would be using that technique instead because all they really care about is how much money they make. Since there isn't a more effective way to sell from the stage, that's the technique they use. They aren't hard closing because they are jerks (although I think they are). They aren't hard closing because they get a kick out of it (although they usually do). They are hard closing because it works better than any other technique out there and all they care about is making money.

I will be the first to tell you I do not have the highest close ratios of a lot of speakers on the circuit. But I can tell you this:

I sleep better than any of them.

I don't care about creating a feeding frenzy in the back of the room, I care about creating loyalty in my relationships with my customers. And when you hard close people and constantly sell without providing any real value, they often regret their decision and eventually cancel anyway.

Now the guilty parties reading this would argue a different perspective. They would say, "Topher doesn't believe in his product as much as I believe in mine. Because if he did, he would want everyone to have his products, like I want people to have mine. Everyone will benefit from my knowledge."

And I would respond, "Really? You're that narcissistic to think EVERYONE needs your product?" I am very proud of the products and services I offer, and I am not so arrogant to think that everyone in the world should buy them And even if someone would benefit from them, it doesn't mean they should buy them immediately without taking into consequence their other financial obligations.

I will happily sacrifice some sales at my events in exchange for peace of mind, knowing that the people who did buy made the right decision, and the people who didn't buy also made the right decision for themselves at that time. This is one of my key beliefs that I share with my clients who hire me to train them as a professional speaker.

If you want to learn the best way to sell from the stage, then go to a training program that specializes in selling from the stage and doesn't focus on the more important aspects of **creating value, connecting with your audience, creating unforgettable experiences, and operating your business with a conscience**. Those four aspects to speaking are what I prefer to focus on. And yes, I even teach how to sell from the stage as well, but it's a technique I've developed over the past 20 years that allows you to incorporate the four key aspects of a professional speaker at the same time. You may not make as much money using my techniques, but the money you make will be clean, and you'll sleep really sound at night.

If you like what you heard and would like to learn some more, then please visit: www.tophersbook.com/7Secrets

By the way, there is a definitive difference between the sleazy hard-selling technique, and using your sales skills to influence potential customers or clients. If someone expresses an interest in your product or service, sharing their need for clarification or the all too common phrase, "I think this is great, except…" by all means use your skill set to help them make the right decision. I'll address that in Section 3, Behind the Desk, in the chapter entitled, Selling Your Seminars.

"How Much Is Too Much?"

At the end of the day, the speaking business is still a business, and if you can't sell effectively, you won't be able to get your message into the minds of those who need it. There is a delicate balance between providing so much content that they don't have a desire to learn any more vs.

providing so little content because you were selling from the stage the entire time. Find this balance and you will have high sales while still being able to sleep at night. Ideally, you want to provide enough content during a presentation that they are happy with their investment of their time, but still hungry for more. You may think giving them massive amounts of content is the best way to provide value, but the reality is, if you do this, you will probably just overwhelm them with data and they won't know the most important points that they should incorporate into their lives.

In the context of selling from the stage, there are usually two extremes you will see in speakers: Those who provide so much value and great content that the participant can't possibly digest all of the information and those who create a seminar/keynote with the sole intention of making a sale and could care less if the participants actually walk away learning anything, they just care about them walking away after buying something.

Finding the sweet spot somewhere in between these two dynamics is a rarity amongst speakers, but what I will encourage you to do.

The challenge with the first type of speaker is that they design their programs with what they have to share in mind, and rarely create programs with how much a participant can actually learn at any one time. They think if they give their audience an incredible amount of information up front, they will be so blown away at this initial talk, surely this audience will want to buy more to continue the journey. But what seems like simple, common knowledge to the speaker who has immersed themselves in their own philosophies for several years can sometimes be such a huge shift in thinking for the audience that they have a hard time grasping the entirety of the concepts being taught.

When designing your training keep this in mind: Giving massive content upfront isn't always giving the best value. Ask yourself these questions when designing your presentations.

1. Out of everything I have to share, what is the most critical?
2. If the participants walked away learning only one thing, what would that be?
3. What are my favorite parts about what I have to teach? And what must they know before they can appreciate the part I love so much?
4. Which parts are connected to encouraging sales?

The answers to these questions will keep you on track in your speech-writing process. Also, when creating your presentation, set your mind to think in phases. In other words, don't create just a seminar, create an anthology of learnings. By breaking your body of knowledge down into more palatable sizes, it creates an easier entry point into your program. In other words, more people will be able to attend a one-day program or even a one-hour program than there will be people who will attend a 10-day program. Once they receive great value at your first course, they will be more inclined find value in investing in your follow-up services, which initially may have been too big of a commitment.

The same tenants for individual sales still apply when selling from the stage: The more you talk about the benefits and the less you speak about the features, the more sales you will generate.

Features

These are the things you teach in your seminar. For example: I used to offer an intensive speaker training course called Legacy. It consisted of 26 traits and techniques that the most influential speakers throughout history have used to inspire the masses. Here are just three:

- Short Stopping
- Projecting Authenticity
- The Charisma Pattern

How inspired do you feel to drop $20,000 for my training right now? Probably not very inspired. The reason you aren't motivated is because these features have no connection to your personal benefit or value. In other words, most likely, your brain hasn't found a way to connect these three phrases to fulfilling your financial and emotional value that you must receive when attending such a course.

Benefits

As a professional speaker, it's our job to take the three phrases listed above, or any features in our programs for that matter, into a place where the audience member can easily create a vivid image in their mind of a potential benefit. Here are the exact three features listed above, in the same order, but this time, from a place of the benefits, not the features.

- There are only two people in the world who can't learn anything: those who know everything, and even worse, those who think they know everything. As a speaker, one of the greatest frustrations on stage is having someone in the audience constantly interjecting their opinion, and even stealing your thunder as they blurt out a lesson that you're building up for. By having the know-it-all change into someone that doesn't-know-it-all, it transforms them into the silent participant eager to learn. By having them transform into the doesn't-know-it-all identity, you will stay on course with your mission in life and reach their mind giving them what they came for—transformation.

- Imagine having an idea that you are so passionate about you want to share it with the world. In fact, not just share it, but have it become a way of life for hundreds, thousands, or perhaps even millions of people around the world. Now imagine having the platform to share that message but people don't trust you. Why wouldn't they? Because believing in an idea is not enough. You must make sure that you are projecting authenticity. No one likes a hypocrite. People don't believe a liar. What's disheartening though is when someone truly believes in something, but because of a few simple errors in presenting that idea, it comes across as inauthentic, and people don't act on the idea. There is something you can do and a way you can speak both verbally and non-verbally that will increase your level of authenticity and create an unshakeable level of conviction in your presentation so when people see it, they hunger for the source of that realism.

- Authenticity is essential; it will get people to believe in you. And even having people believe in you is not enough nowadays. You must create a desire to follow you. And I don't mean create a bunch of followers; I mean create a bunch of doers. Too many people just talk the talk these days. What we need more of are people who are willing to walk the walk. Imagine having the same level of charisma that Barack Obama used to win over 97% of the world in his favor before the election. Imagine being so charismatic as to inspire thousands to walk like Martin Luther King, Jr. did. Charisma isn't about good looks, size, or stature; it's an intangible quality that can be created through four tangible and easy-to-apply ways of communicating.

Now at this point, you still may not be willing to invest $20,000 into my training program, but even the most sales-resistant person would be more curious about the program than when I simply said that I teach Short Stopping, Projecting Authority, and The Charisma Pattern. This should be your goal: to increase the audience's curiosity about what you are selling. If properly done, they won't feel sold; they'll feel inspired to take action.

CHAPTER 11

HOW POWERFUL ARE YOUR POINTS?

There are many facets that make up a successful professional speaker. Some of them are related to how you run your business; others are related to how you perform as a speaker. One major component in your performance is how you put a slide presentation to use.

Why do professional speakers use slides in the first place? Ideally, the main function of a slide is to enhance the audience's experience of learning. Slides help communicate something visually that would take much longer to verbally express. They point out important facts worthy of remembering. Remember this basic tenant when designing your slides: only put on the slides what you want them to remember. When Steve Jobs unveiled the MacBook Air in 2008, the slide he used had a picture of an inner-office envelope. That's it. And we all got it. It's the world's thinnest laptop. So thin, it can fit in an envelope.

I could write an entire book on all of the intricacies for a powerful slide presentation: What colors work best? How much text should go on a slide? Should you have animations? What copyright laws relate to photographs and movies? Should you use sound effects on your slides? Where are the best places to get pre-designed slides? Should you even use pre-designed slides? What kind of remote controls are the best? Which is better, front or rear projection? Which is better, PowerPoint, Keynote, or Prezi? The list goes on and on.

In the near 30 years I've been a professional speaker, I've noticed certain things come up year after year, time after time, that make a presentation weaker. When speakers include these things in their PowerPoint slides, it often turns their audience off and make it hard for them to hear what the presenter is really trying to say to them. The good news is that these mistakes are quick and easy to fix.

The 3 Worst Things in Your Slides
1. PICTURES OF YOURSELF

Being a speaker is a very strange profession. People pay to have you tell stories about your lives, but in reality, they don't really care about you. They only care about themselves. Finding that balance between sharing a life event which has a lesson worth hearing and just talking about your life is a finely defined line. Here is one of those lines:

Contrary to what most speech coaches tell you, you should NEVER have a slide or slides in your presentation that have pictures of you on vacation, being successful, standing in front of your Bentley or boat.

A few years back, I was the featured keynote speaker at a prosperity conference in Sarasota, FL. I arrived a few hours early so I had the opportunity for me to see the speaker before me. His presentation was filled with pictures of him on vacation, standing in front of expensive cars, and rubbing elbows with celebrities. When he started speaking, there were about 60 people in the audience. By the time he was finished there were only 13. What went wrong? He came across as arrogant and self-serving, which turned off the majority of his audience. His purpose of showing the photos was to inspire the audience to buy his products so they, too, could create an amazing life. But since a picture is worth a thousand words and all of his pictures had him in them, the way I calculated it, he had about 200,000 words all about himself! By the very nature of his photos, he accomplished the equivalent of going to a social gathering and talking about himself non-stop.

Make sure the thousand words your pictures reflect in your presentation are the words you want them to hear. Generally, if you are going to use photos in your presentation, leave yourself out and stay with stock photography. There are two reasons for this. Firstly, it allows room in the photo for the audience to place themselves in the picture (if you're in it, there may not be any room for them), and secondly, a picture of yourself will most likely be an amateur photograph and your presentation will immediately reflect that same level of unprofessionalism.

You want your audience to walk away thinking, "I can do that!" In other words, you want them to create very vivid images of them in their head standing in front of their own Bentley, in front of their own mansion, and standing beside the celebrities that they dream about rubbing shoulders with. If they are looking at pictures of you doing that, there isn't any room in that picture for them. Get rid of your ego, and get out of the pictures so your audience can find the space for them to occupy their own dreams.

So why do people feel the need to use these slides? Because they have been told that they have to make sure the audience respects them and sees them as credible. That's all well and good, and I agree that a bit of respect goes a long way. But take the sophisticated road and build your credibility with class.

2. MORE TEXT THAN PICTURES

The audience is there to listen to you speak. If they want to read something, they can buy your book. Too many speakers fill their slides with way too many steps in bullet point format, and paragraphs that look like they are writing the next Harry Potter novel. Audiences are conditioned to write down whatever they see on a slide. If you have too much text on your slide, the audience will spend too much time writing down word for word what is on your slide, and they won't even hear what you are saying. Words on slides are best if they are conceptual or induce questions in the audience's mind, the answers of which will be the solutions to their problems.

Unfortunately, most speakers simply use their slides as a cheat sheet for what they are talking about. They use it to help them remember what they are saying. Now I'd be lying if I said I've never used slides for this purpose, so I'm certainly not casting any stones, but the quality of my presentations are far better when the slides are not a crutch, but rather, a compliment. How can you ensure they are compliments instead of crutches? You must do two things: memorize your slides, and memorize your presentation. If you are constantly looking at the slides while you are speaking, you will look unprepared, and you will be unprofessional. If you constantly keep your eye contact with the audience, and move through your slides without ever having to look at them, yet you are still talking about them, your audience will be impressed without realizing why. There will be something different about you than from other speakers they've seen and it can come down to something as simple as this one artistic tactic of never having to look at your own slides.

Click here for a demonstration on the power of this affect: www.tophersbook.com/slidemem

According to the seminal essay by George Miller, published by "Psychological Review" in 1956, people have a hard time remembering more than seven unrelated pieces of data at once. Anything more than that and a person may begin to feel a sense of overwhelm. This study says nothing about a human's ability to remember something on a visual aid. So when speaking schools tell you to limit the amounts of information on a slide to no more than 7 (at most 9) pieces of information, they are making those claims based on misunderstood information. There is absolutely no scientific data that reinforces this claim; however, common sense does. It only makes sense that the more information you put on a slide, the more information someone will try to remember. The less they remember, the more they might begin to feel overwhelmed with the information.

So keep it simple and keep it clean. A lot of open space on a slide makes the visual aid "breathable" and is visually more comfortable to the eye.

There is a more important reason to keep your slides simple. When you are speaking, you want your audience listening. If they are busy transcribing never-ending amounts of data on a slide presentation, they will not be listening to what you are saying, and what's worse, when you want to transition to the next slide, someone who is slow at taking notes will inevitably raise their hand and ask you to slow down, back up a slide, or halt your presentation until they have written down everything you have put on your slide. If the information is that important and that detailed, then you should probably have some sort of training manual accompanying your presentation, and the information should be in there. Remember, your audience will write down everything you put on a slide, so limit what you put on the slide or they will never stop writing, and never begin listening.

3. WORDS OR PICTURES WITHOUT ANY CONTRAST

Speakers invariably design their slides on a PC or laptop. The contrast on an LED screen is beautiful and crisp. It's easy to read when the screen is only 20 inches from your nose. But when those slides are projected onto a screen from a projector, which, in most cases, is old, outdated, and weak in brightness, the pictures dissolve into indiscernible shapes, the text disappears into the background, and what's left is a speaker saying something to the effect of, *"Well you can't really see it on the screen, but this is a picture of.…"* Or they have to read all the text to the audience, which then turns into the annoying task of repeating yourself until the slowest writer in the room has written down everything you have said for the 20th time. This is easily fixed by one of two strategies.

First, once you have designed a slide, scoot your chair back until you are about 10 feet away from your screen. Can you still make out the images and text easily? If not, you need to make some visual changes in the presentation.

Second, and most important, design your slide presentation using a projector plugged into your computer. This will eliminate any surprises later.

Lastly, we need to address the quality of the pictures used in a presentation as well. When selecting pictures for your slide presentations, there are usually two roads to take. Which road you choose will determine your level of professionalism or lack thereof. The amateur speaker uses Google Images and essentially steals the artistic property of someone else. In the beginning, a lot of speakers try saving money, but is saving money really worth sacrificing your integrity and moral code? With information so readily available online, it's getting easier and easier to download video and pictures from someone else without their permission. Just because someone has their information posted in the public domain does not mean that you are given permission to use it. In some instances, this may not be illegal, but in the cases where it is, remember this: It's still stealing. Beyond the moral implications of stealing other people's property, there is the professional impression to consider as well. A picture downloaded from Google Images may be low-resolution and when inserted into a slide presentation may be pixilated and low quality. I've even seen some people have pictures in their slides that still have the watermark or copyright infringement warnings on them! Many speakers try saving money by using their own photos as well, and rarely do these have the quality to create a good impression. Once again, this will reflect poorly on you.

The road less traveled would be the road a professional speaker takes. Purchase pictures from a stock photography website. This ensures that you have the highest quality resolution, and the legal right to use it. There are two sites that I highly recommend. If you are going to need a large quantity of pictures, www.gettyimages.com has a membership site that allows you to pay for unlimited downloads each month. This is far more cost effective when you are getting started. If you are only going to need a few pictures occasionally, then I recommend www.istockphoto.com.

For most of your work, these two sites will be able to adequately provide all of the background and emotion-based pictures you will need.

If you would like to see some samples of slides that I've used in the past incorporating this information, go to www.slideshare.net and search for my name. I've created a specific slide show for this very chapter. Feel free to take a look at Powerful Points. I'm always adding more slideshows so make sure to go back from time to time and see what new information is there.

CHAPTER 12

PUTTING IT ALL TOGETHER

ll of the techniques you've learned about in the previous chapters will polish the diamond, but what makes sure you have a diamond to start with? Let's face it, the best techniques in the world, applied to a presentation that is fundamentally flawed right from the beginning, will never give you the sense of pride and accomplishment you strive for as a speaker, because when you walk off the stage you will feel like "something was missing."

I've seen some speakers get up and present to a room full of people, and they are essentially following the majority, if not all of the techniques outlined in the previous chapters and yet it's a lack-luster presentation. It falls short. The audience never fully connects. They seem a bit random or unprepared and it never really makes the impact I believe they truly wanted. The reasons for this vary, but there is one common flaw that the majority of these speakers fall prey to. They base their entire presentation on four very dangerous words any speaker could say. If you have ever said these words, please read this brief, but powerful chapter more than once. Make a personal commitment never to have to say this phrase ever again. **One of the worst phrases a speaker could ever say about their upcoming presentation is "I'll just wing it."**

I could write an entire book on why this is a terrible attitude, but you really only need to accept this one concept. When you "just wing it" during a presentation, you are being disrespectful to the audience, the organizer of the event, the information you are going to share, the profession of the speaking industry, and most of all, you are disrespecting yourself. Be better than that. Treat yourself, and those who hear your presentation with the care and respect everyone deserves.

Think about it. How would you feel as a customer if you brought your car to the mechanic and they said, "I'll just wing it. I'll call you once I've figured it all out and done whatever it is I'm going to do"? How about a veterinarian for your beloved pet? "Not sure what's wrong, but I'll just wing it and you can pick your pet up tomorrow." You have to appear in court, you ask your attorney, "Do you feel optimistic about the case?" and they respond with, "Oh yeah, I mean, who knows how this thing will actually turn out, but I'm just going to get up there and wing it." A wedding planner? "Hey good luck on your wedding today, regarding the reception, I just thought I would wing it and see what happens." No respectable professional in any career would have a good reputation if they chose to "just wing it." And this part of your profession should be no different.

I Won't Just Wing It

It begins by making sure you have taken the time to hone your presentations and that they are delivered with professionalism and grace. This single factor is what I think separates one's ability to shift from a public speaker to somebody who can generate financial rewards and become a professional speaker. "I'll just wing it" is the mark of an amateur. It's usually begins by someone going to a seminar, seeing someone on stage and thinking, "That doesn't seem too difficult. She just gets up there and talks. I want to do that, too." Bang! Another public speaker is born.

I've heard every excuse in the book from speakers who say they don't want to have a prepared and rehearsed presentation, but the most common one is, "I don't like to sound rehearsed, I just like to have the presentation unfold organically." What they fail to realize is that the best speakers out there, those who create the appearance of their presentations unfolding organically (whatever the heck that means) have a structured outline that they are following. Their preparation gives them the flexibility to then play off the audience. It's very much like a stage magician who has several tricks available depending upon what happens from the audience—it may seem all spontaneous, but make no mistake, they have covered all their bases of possibility, and that's what a professional speaker must do as well. To quote one of the greatest and most successful professional speakers of all time, Zig Ziglar: "If your presentation sounds canned, you haven't canned your presentation."

The other reason people say they don't want to have a memorized presentation is that they say it prevents them from connecting with their audience because they are trying to present a memorized speech. Fair enough. But if you're trying to remember it when you are on stage, I would submit you aren't fully prepared. Wanting to connect with your audience is the exact reason why you want to can your presentation. Once you have completely memorized your entire presentation so much so that you can present it in your sleep, forward and backward, you no longer have to focus on what you are saying, and you have the ability then to truly connect with your audience. If you are "winging it," then you are constantly going back in your head to orchestrate the best way to say something.

How much time should you spend rehearsing your presentations? The industry standard for a world-class presenter is around **20 hours of rehearsal time for every five minutes on stage**. Remember that the next time you think how easy it is to just get up and talk to a crowd. If you aren't willing to commit the time necessary to master your presentation, most likely, the big bucks will always elude you.

I'm always amused when I see "Train the Trainer" programs that teach people how to present in a weekend. Would you entrust your car to a person who was a certified mechanic after one weekend? How about taking your dog to a vet that got their certification in three days? A lawyer? A pharmacist? How about a CEO? "No, I don't have any actual CEO experience, but I went to a weekend seminar teaching me how to do it." You wouldn't be attracted to working with any of these types of professions with minimal training, and being a professional speaker is no different.

That is not meant to discount the quality of some weekend workshops. However, just because you attend a weekend workshop, it doesn't mean you are now ready to get up on stage and start being compensated for your presentations. It's the starting point— and the best ones will tell you that and offer some sort of ongoing mentorship support to help you on your journey. Workshops are not the ending point. Out of all the weekend workshops I've seen, there is one that stands out above all the rest: The Bill Gove Speech Workshop. It's the perfect starting point for a business leader who wants to become more effective as a presenter and leave their audiences wanting more. They offer programs worldwide, always sell out, and usually have a waiting list to get in, so if you are at all curious, I would call them now to start looking at dates and locations.

Feel free to tell them I sent you! Here's a shortcut to their site: www.tophersbook.com/siebold

The Evolution of Spontaneity

So how do the world's best speakers create that level of spontaneity, which secretly is completely rehearsed? There are two main ways and one of them is becoming quickly outdated:

First, you master your presentation by giving your presentation hundreds of times. This allows for less rehearsal time as you are primarily practicing on stage. You know that a speaker is using this strategy when you attend their speech more than once and each time you attend it is significantly different than the time before. Usually one time it's great, the other time it's lackluster. This technique is becoming more and more obsolete because there are more speakers out there than ever, which means competition is greater than ever and that you can't afford to go through a mediocre phase in front of your audience. If you do, they'll just move on to the next speaker. By my count there are currently three world-class, world-renowned speakers who are using this technique, and their success is waning fast.

The second technique is what got so many people to Carnegie Hall: "Practice, practice, practice." I can't give you one definitive right way to do this, but I can share with you my personal strategy. I don't even follow my own strategy all the time, but when I do, I knock it out of the park every single time.

Phase 1—I script out the entire presentation word for word. Yes, it's arduous. Yes, it's tedious. Yes, there are a million other things I would rather be doing because it's very time-consuming. But when it's all said and done, rarely will you ever have to go back and re-read what you wrote word for word during rehearsal. By writing it out word for word, you can craft the message so precisely that you will know that your speech is sending the message you want and nothing more. The message, at this phase, is essentially "perfect." Now move onto phase II—Wreck it.

Short Cut—Instead of sitting down and writing out a 45-minute, one-day, or even multi-day event all at once, keep a journal with you at all times (my new journal is in the form of an iPhone) and when you have some free time, begin writing out individual vignettes that drive home a specific point. Compile them into a log and then when you need the right story for the lesson you are creating, it's already pre-created. This technique was taught to me by Steve Siebold, one of the best professional speaking coaches I've ever had the pleasure of knowing. It's an honor for me to call him my friend, my colleague, and my mentor. If you are ever wondering if you should attend any of his trainings, stop wondering, and cut the check.

And if you would like to see an interview I did with Steve to learn some of the Bill Gove system, check out this interview here: www.tophersbook.com/steveint.

Phase II—Wreck it. Go back, and in the script, put in the flaws. The "ums" at the right place, the "self-corrections." All the things that make normal speech, well, normal. Your goal is not to become one of those perfectly groomed speakers who never stumble, and run through their presentation flawlessly. That creates a disconnect with the audience and they will either have a hard time relating to you or, even worse, put you on a pedestal and make the huge mistake of thinking you're perfect.

Phase III—Break down the presentation into main thought points and give them a label. This label becomes your one-word cue to what the entire story is all about. Take those labels and place the key words and phrases below it that you want to make sure you communicate.

Phase IV—Read the entire script aloud as if you were presenting it in real time. Stand up and do this with stopwatch in hand and note the start and end time of every section of the presentation. Continue to rehearse the presentation until you can come within 30 seconds every time of the original start and stop time. If you are off further than 30 seconds, go back to re-reading the script word for word until it is engrained in your brain.

Phase V—Rewrite the outline with only the one-word label and the start time and end time. Continue to rehearse the presentation. making sure you can hit every cue within 30 seconds of the written time. If not, go back to the previous outline that has the key words and phrases to keep on track. Once you can present the speech within 5 - 15 seconds of the time written, then you know you've canned it and will now have the flexibility to improvise, play around, and connect with your audience when delivering it for real.

Push Through the Dip

Seth Godin wrote a powerful book called "The Dip—A Little Book That Teaches You When to Quit (And when to Stick)." He describes the dip as the long stretch between beginner's luck and real accomplishment. After reading this chapter, you might all too easily think, "But Topher, I've already done presentations where I winged the whole thing and the audience loved it." Yep. I get that. It can happen. And I would attribute that to one or two things—probably a little of both. #1. Beginner's Luck. #2. Reread the intro of this book; specifically the section called, "How Great to You Really Need to Be?" Your audience wasn't a room full of skeptics. In fact, I'd be willing to bet a handful of them were your friends or colleagues, and they were the people praising you at the end.

Pushing through the dip is what you will need to do in order to achieve the level of excellence you know in your heart you are capable of. The five phases of rehearsal described previously in this chapter are the key to pushing through the dip. It's hard. Not everyone will do it. When faced with the dip, most people get lazy and quit. Those people are average. And to quote Seth, "The next time you catch yourself being average when you feel like quitting, realize that you have only two good choices: Quit or be exceptional. Average is for losers." Don't be average. Trust me, when you are preparing for a presentation you'll want to quit. Many times. You'll come up with tons of excuses on why you don't have time to rehearse. All of those excuses are for the average.

Most people who want to get up and speak do so because they fundamentally feel that the knowledge they have could benefit others. Isn't that true for you? If so, why wouldn't you do everything you can to ensure the knowledge you impart is delivered in the most compelling way possible to make sure that as many people as possible walk away from your talk inspired, and ready to implement their newfound wisdom into action?

PART 2

ON CAMERA

CHAPTER 13

INTERVIEWING SKILLS

Y ou might be tempted to just skip over this entire section if you feel that you have no need or desire to interview experts in areas that you speak about, or topics that might compliment what you do. That would be a mistake. People consume information at an alarming rate—much faster than they used to. Thirty years ago, you could write a book about a subject, like "The 7 Habits of Highly Effective People" and make an entire career out of those 7 points, and one book. It was 25 years later that Stephen Covey wrote his second book, "The 8th Habit: From Effectiveness to Greatness."

Good luck speaking for 25 years about the same topic without any additional content in today's environment. People will get tired of you, and someone next month will come up with something more innovative than what you are talking about today. It's safe to say that even the most innovative, forward-thinking speakers today cannot keep up with the consumption rate of their fan base. This is why the most prolific speakers are reaching out to other thought leaders and sharing with their fan base the ideas of others. Interviewing other experts is an essential piece to your professional speaking career.

The good news is, as a professional speaker, you will attract many opportunities to partner with other thought leaders. These opportunities can, if done correctly, become life-changing. If done poorly, this will result in your audience walking out of the room during live interviews; and when broadcasting your video online, will result in people clicking off to watch videos of people crashing on motorcycles, cats playing the piano, or whatever mindless vids happen to be more entertaining than you.

Sometimes you will be on the guest side of the interview, other times, you might be on the host side interviewing another expert in their field. It's important to understand the responsibilities of both sides so you are fully prepared in any situation. So in this section, I'll cover the skills of interviewing first, then tips on how to be a great guest on someone else's show.

These interviews may be on camera, stage, radio, or podcast. The majority of the skills work across all platforms and if you can become proficient in one, you will most likely feel at ease in all of the other formats. The most important one is TV. Once you've mastered this, all the other platforms can very quickly become second nature.

Be the Hostess with the Mostest

When you are the host of an interview, it is 100% your responsibility to make sure that the interview is entertaining, insightful, engaging, and keeps the listener listening or the viewer watching. If the old adage, "there are no bad kids, only bad parents" is true, then for public speaking, there are no bad guests, only bad hosts.

Some guests make your job super easy. They talk in succinct sound bites, they are engaging and fun to listen to. Others are about as exciting as oatmeal and talk at the same speed and consistency. But it doesn't matter. When you get a great guest you are lucky, when you have a bad guest, you have to work. Follow these techniques and you can take the worst guest and turn the interview into something worth sharing.

Remember this: After an interview, a professional host will never say, "What a lousy guest." A great host will say, "Well, they made me work, but we still pulled off a great interview." That is your goal. Set your benchmark for success on how you as the host delivered, not how your guest performed.

You Are Their First Impression

Before the guest even says one word, your introduction is going to set the tone. They don't set their first impression; you do. Do not leave this to chance or wing it, and whatever you do, don't have them introduce themselves. I'll explain why in the section below, Don't Get Lazy. Ask them to provide you with an introduction, but don't read it word for word. If they don't provide you with an introduction, get online, do your homework (or if you have a producer, have them do the homework), collect the most exciting points, and welcome them to the interview by presenting them in the best light possible.

To do that, don't read an intro word for word—especially if they wrote it! This never sounds authentic. In fact, it's quite obvious to the audience members that the guest wrote the intro, they might as well have been the one to read it at that point. Read through the intro several times, and have most of the content committed to memory so you don't sound stiff or canned in the intro. And here's the one magic tip to make an introduction feel authentic, original, and create the impression that you are excited to have that guest on your show: Insert a personal story about you and the guest. This makes it personal. It makes your guest human and easier to trust. It allows the audience that already trusts you and associates their feelings to yours to immediately feel connected to the guest.

That personal story does not have to be something from your childhood, 10 years ago, or even a year ago. The story could be something that happened 10 minutes ago before you both came on stage or got in front of the camera. Tell the audience something personal about that guest that you admire or love about them. You'll be amazed at how much more responsive your audience will be and how much more comfortable you will make your guest feel when they start the interview.

What if you didn't have any personal interaction with the guest? Maybe they are a celebrity who just shows up after your show has already begun and the first interaction you have with them is on air? While unlikely, you can still apply this technique, but instead of telling the audience a personal interaction story about you and the guest, pull something from their introduction that means something to you personally and share with your audience why you think that is important, or share how that person has impacted your life in a positive way. The effect will be the same, and your interview will start off on a much higher note.

Don't Get Lazy

Avoid phrases like, "tell the audience about yourself," "tell me more about that," or, "How can people get a hold of you?" These types of questions are lazy. They put the responsibility of a good show on the guest and, in the case of that last question, make them have to pimp their goods and services on your show which never feels good. You're the host. You should know how someone can get a hold of them, and proudly broadcast that. You should know where they can get a copy of their book, and tell your audience exactly where to get it. Don't abdicate that responsibility back to your guest.

Instead, have their contact information readily available. Have their bio close at hand so you can introduce them properly. Have questions about their bio, their past, present, and future all mapped out and ready to go. It doesn't mean you won't ask other questions, you should, but have a baseline of starting questions that get the ball rolling and make them feel at ease. Let them answer questions they already know the answer to. "Tell us about yourself" just panics the guest and they don't know what is important to share, and as a result, they might bumble and fumble around with no end game in mind. They don't look good, you don't look good, and people check out of the interview. Instead, ask them a specific question like "You were raised in British Columbia, that place is beautiful! What kind of things did a kid in Kelowna do for fun back then?" Now they have a direction and it's much easier for them to answer.

And when they answer the question, LISTEN TO THE ANSWER! Don't be stepping ahead to the next question in your mind. If you do, you'll make a fool out of yourself because eventually they will say something in the answer to your first question that clearly answers the second question without you ever having to ask it. If you now just throw out the second question because you weren't listening to the answer in the first question, they will have to either repeat themselves, or even worse, tell you they just answered that question 10 seconds ago, making you look like an idiot.

In an ideal interview, the second question should come as a result of something they said in the first answer. The third question should come as a result of something from the second answer, and so on. If you aren't listening, this can't happen. But when you are listening, it allows you to dig deeper than other interviewers and guests love that!

Dig Baby Dig!

When interviewing your guest, the easiest thing to do is ask the questions they provide you. While that might be an okay starting point, it will rarely be the bulk of a great interview. One of the reasons for this is most guests (including myself) will typically create questions that are self-serving. The questions advance their own agenda and position them to talk about their expertise. And while you want to cover some of that information in an interview, rarely will the information they are an expert in be the most intriguing or entertaining portion of the interview. You might be thinking, "I don't care if I'm entertaining, I want to educate and inform." Please go back and re-read the chapter 4, **"Crank It Up."**

The information age is dead. The collaboration age is upon us and people care more about *who* you are than *what* you know. In fact, in today's age, people will often do business with you based more on *who* you are over *what* your qualifications are. Today *what* is passé, *who* is relevant. So focus more on *who* they are than *what* they know. Dig into their thoughts, their feelings, what they have learned in their lifetime. It's one thing to find out what they believe and what upsets them, but even more importantly, people want to know why they believe it and why it upsets them.

You will, of course, still need to have some information inside the interview. You will want to dedicate some time to what they know—what they are an expert in. But even asking those questions can be handled with strategy to make them far more entertaining of an interview. Here's the key:

Don't ask the question; ask the question behind the question.

The "question" is the most obvious question. It's probably the list of questions they provided you before the interview. And, if they are a common guest on shows, they are the same questions that they have provided every other interviewer. This is a problem, because it means that these answers are most likely already somewhere on the internet in one form or another—video, audio, or print. So when you ask the questions every other host has already asked, you get the same answers and it becomes predictable and boring.

John Heffron, my friend and co-author of "I Come to You from the Future," won The Last Comic Standing in 2004. After his win, he was interviewed all over the country on TV and radio. He shared that one of the first questions the majority of hosts asked him was, "What did it feel like when you won?" That's a great example of the obvious question. It's not very original, as demonstrated by the fact that the majority of the hosts asked it. This very quickly would send him on auto-pilot. Instead of wanting to stay on air and entertain, John would wonder how fast he could get off the interview and on to the next one. Until one special interview. The host actually asked John if he was annoyed by how many people had been asking him what it felt like to win. That is the question behind the question. Immediately John was reengaged, he wanted to have a great conversation, he wanted to stick around and banter back and forth with the host. The host asked a question that wasn't obvious and brought out a sense of play and creativity than none of the other interviews did.

The question behind the question is the one that isn't obvious. It's the deeper piece behind the obvious question, and often is the question nobody else has the courage, sense of adventure, or care to ask. But if you look at the greatest interviewers of all time, those are the kinds of questions they ask. Watch Oprah, Ellen DeGeneres, Jon Stewart, Graham Norton, or Howard Stern; study the greats like Barbara Walters, Walter Cronkite, or Larry King. These professional speakers are amazing when it comes to interviewing their guests. They dig deep; they ask questions most people would never have the courage to ask, but they consistently are recognized in the field as some of the best in what they do.

So how do you ask the questions behind the questions? Start by writing out the questions you want to ask. Or look at the list of questions the guest provides. Then ask yourself any of these questions and the answers to these questions will become the gateway to you discovering the question behind the question:

"What's beyond this question?"

"What's their motivation for wanting me to ask this question?"

"What's REALLY going on here?"

"What part of the answer to this question would they not want me to pursue?"

"What do I want to know about them that I could never ask?"

There are many more of these kinds of initiator questions, and I think you get the idea. Your job as the host of an interview is to think of the questions that nobody else has considered, or would have the courage to ask. When you do that, you've probably hit the question behind the question.

Yes or No, That isn't the Question

There are two types of questions you can ask in an interview: closed-ended questions which require a simple yes or no answer or open-ended questions encouraging the guest to engage in a dialogue and share something interesting. It seems obvious that you would want to ask open-ended questions, and in most cases, that is the best strategy, but it does have its drawbacks. The biggest is that you lose control of the interview once you ask an open-ended question. It's difficult to control how long they will take to answer, and whether or not they will even answer the question in the way you had hoped to set up your anticipated next question.

So if you find yourself running out of time, asking an open-ended question may result in you going longer than allowed. As you find yourself getting closer to the end of your interview, switching to a closed-ended question might help you to finish on time. This is why talk show hosts sometimes have segments that force the guest to answer brief questions. A great example of this would be Ken Rutkowski's "Business Rockstars" radio show. He has a segment where he puts 60 seconds on the clock and asks a series of closed-ended questions like, "Who is your favorite entrepreneur?" "The Matrix or Dumb & Dumber?" "What's your favorite animal?" "What's the latest book you read?" "Apple or PC?"

Closed-ended questions are also a great way to regain control if you have a guest who tends to ramble on and rarely get to the point. If you have this type of guest, you can interrupt after a period of time (usually 30 seconds) and ask them a closed-ended question. This immediately stops the ramble and lets you get on to the next question. For example, let's say you ask your guest a question about their proudest moment as a father, and they start by saying, "When I was little boy, I remember my parents telling me…" You already know this is a ramble, because you asked them a question about their adulthood and they are starting back at their childhood. This could be a show killer. Wait for them to get to a place in their ramble where you can ask them a closed-ended question and butt in. Maybe it could sound something like this, "… which of your parents do you think you turned out more like, your Mom or Dad?" This forces them to refocus, give you a one-word answer, and then you can continue on with a new question, hopefully related to a parenting joke or story so it doesn't seem too abrupt. But even if it is abrupt, don't panic. It's perfectly okay, the best interviewers frequently change direction, butt in, and redirect the conversation.

The Best Interviewers Have the Best Butts

It's not just enough to have great questions; one critical component to a great interview is knowing when to ask the questions. And the best answer I can give you would be to ask the next question before they have finished answering the first one. That's right. Butt in. Interrupt them and don't let them finish their train of thought. "But that would be rude!" you say. Really? Sit back at your next lunch with a group of people. Just listen to the conversation. You'll discover that almost everything said at the table is the result of someone butting in on the other person. It's how natural conversation happens. The only people who ask a question, allow for an awkward gap in-between, listen to the full answer, only to have another awkward gap are interviewers from National Public Radio. That, and almost every boring podcast you've ever listened to.

Does this mean you butt in every single time? Probably, but don't make it a contest either. If they finish an answer and you haven't butted in, it's not the end of the world. Just ask your next question as quickly as you can to eliminate as much 'dead air' as possible.

Now the topic of the butt-in is as important as the butt-in itself. If you simply railroad your guest and ask a bunch of unrelated questions, it's going to come across rude and probably make you look like you aren't listening, or don't care about what they are saying. But if you butt-in with a question about something they just said, the opposite happens. It shows you are listening, and you really do care because you want to go deeper in their topic.

Who's Late for the Party?

If your interview is longer than 15 minutes, it's a good idea to reintroduce your guest several times. The only time where this might be a bit strange would be at a non-televised live interview in front of an audience. But every other time, you should assume people will be tuning into the interview late, and you'll need to get them caught up to speed.

A general rule of thumb would be reintroduce your guest every time you come back from break, or every 15 minutes if there are no places for interruptions. And it's as simple as saying something like, "for those of you just tuning in, we've got [insert name] in the studio. She's an expert in [this thing] and here to share with us today how we can do it better." And the best time to do that is when they complete an answer without you interrupting and you shift focus for a brief moment, reintroduce, then get right back into your questions.

CHAPTER 14

GUEST SKILLS

B eing a guest is always a fun experience, especially if you have a great host. But regardless of how good or bad the host is, it's 100% your responsibility to make sure that the interview is entertaining, insightful, engaging, and keeps the listener listening or the viewer watching. Yes, I realize I wrote the same words about the host during the interviewer chapter. But now you're the guest, so you better be a good one. And for several reasons. The first of which is you want that host to ask you back again. That won't happen if you are a boring guest who answers the questions in short "yes" or "no" answers and is the auditory equivalent of a bowl of oatmeal. No, I don't have anything against oatmeal; in fact I like it, but I don't want to interview it. Don't be oatmeal.

Know Your Outcome

You must know why you are being interviewed. Is it to sell your products or services? Is it to entertain the audience? Is it to get more credibility? Are you going for fame and fortune? I suppose the list could go on for days, but as I see it, there really are only two main reasons why anyone would take time out of their productive day to be interviewed by someone on TV, radio, or a podcast.

#1. To raise your profile, gain credibility

#2. To sell your product or service

When I am a guest on a TV or radio show, I prefer option #1, and I would encourage you to do the same. For podcasts, I may be a bit more self-serving as typically listeners of podcasts are looking for solutions more than trying to be entertained. This is very strategic and usually has a better payoff when appearing on TV or radio. You might be thinking, "I want to do both!" That's a great ambition; it's also a strategy for failure. These outcomes are mutually exclusive. You can't have both so you have to pick. That's not to say that if you raise your profile on a show you won't get any business. You might just get lucky, but to have both as an outcome rarely, if ever. pays off.

Raising Your Profile, Gain Credibility

It's amazing how much credibility people give guests on television shows, especially nationally syndicated ones. The moment you are featured on CNN, Fox News, the BBC, or World Asia, you are seen as an authority in your field. But to have any of these major national networks call you and ask for an interview is next to impossible unless you've killed someone.

So how do you get featured on these shows? Similar to how a professional athlete makes it into the major leagues: you work your way up through the ranks. Before a national news network or syndicated talk show will feel comfortable having you on air, they will want to know you can handle the stress of cameras and lights focused all on you. So they will look to see if you've had any airtime on local shows in smaller markets. If you can provide them footage to those shows, and they see that you are engaging, entertaining, and a great guest, they will be more inclined to book you.

How do you get onto a local show? They will often ask you to supply footage as well, because they have the same concerns as a national network might. Have you been featured on a cable access show? That will work! Do you have any footage on YouTube or any of the other internet video channels? That will work! And that's the great thing about cable access shows. They have virtually no filters for letting you on air. Most of the time, they are starved for guests and will book you sight unseen. As for YouTube or other internet video channels? Your 12-year-old nephew probably has his own channel. Anyone can. So you have no excuse for not having your own shows on your own YouTube channel.

I treat every video on YouTube as if it is an audition reel for a local network television or radio show. When I get booked onto those local shows, I treat them as an audition to a nationally syndicated television or radio show. When I'm on a nationally syndicated talk show, I treat that as an audition for getting invited back. I'm always working to earn my way back. When I successfully do that, I've fulfilled my goal of raising my exposure, and I could care less if I sell any of my products or services on the show. That can come in the repurposing of the footage on my website to position myself as the authority on the subject I speak on.

Now beyond using previous footage to assure the booking agents for bigger shows that I'm a safe bet and will be a great guest, the one overriding technique that works better than anything to be invited onto TV and radio is to be a published author. When that happens, you've just cut to the front of the line and increased your chances dramatically.

Selling Your Products

If you have a product or service that you are trying to move, then there is probably no better way than to be featured on TV or a popular radio show. The host doesn't even have to endorse you—your presence on their show is all the endorsement you need to move massive amounts of product. But just being on the show isn't enough to sell, there are specific tips and tricks that the best pitchmen in the world use to sell products through the media.

Don't expect that you can get on air, and just talk about the features of your product. This strategy NEVER works. And if you do that, I can promise you will never be invited back to the show. Even if the person watching or listening to the show actually wants your product, this strategy has proven to produce little to no success. You MUST tell stories that sell your product or services.

What type of stories? The type that will grab the largest amount of viewers or listeners and get them to say to themselves, "Me, too!" These stories must have the basic components I outlined in the chapter, "How to Avoid Living in a Van Down by the River." I covered the notion of Premise, Problem and Solution. Each story you tell needs to be a different premise or problem so that you capture the widest amount of the audience. Some listening might relate to the first story, while others might respond best to your second or third. The idea is to have as many stories ready to go that cover the biggest problems and solutions your product or service delivers. When you do that, the audience listening has a greater chance of saying, "Me too!" and you make a sale. If the audience can't relate to the stories you tell, no matter how entertaining they might be, you won't compel them to place an order.

The Best Guests Have Some Amazing Butts, Too!

Regardless of your outcome, you want to make sure the viewer keeps watching and the listener keeps listening. The host, if they are good, will eliminate the spaces of dead air on their end, but if they ask you a question and you pause to think about the answer, and let a long silent gap overtake the airwaves, you will drastically diminish your level of entertainment value. "But I'm not getting on air to entertain, I'm getting on air to educate." I get that. And if you aren't entertaining, they will click off the station and you won't be able to educate them anyway. So you absolutely must become entertaining as a guest if you want to have the opportunity to educate. Eliminating silent gaps between when you speak and the interviewer posts a question is a simple way to make the interview more entertaining. By the way, if you leave too long of a silent gap, a good host will start talking again and not give you the chance to answer the question you were preparing. They will dig down into a simple yes or no answer to get you to say anything at all, and then they will overtake the interview to keep their audience entertained. Don't believe me? Watch the interview between David Letterman and his guest, Paris Hilton—arguably one of the worst guests on a national talk show ever. It was still entertaining though, not because of her, but because Letterman is an interview host genius. But as a guest? She was a nightmare. Just search "David Letterman Paris Hilton Interview on YouTube. It's there.

So how do you eliminate that silent gap after a host asks a question? Butt-in. Just like they do. If you know where the question is heading, just start answering it. Trust me, the professional host won't care. In fact, they will love it. It will make you more entertaining. For an example of how this looks, you can see a video from my interview on the Daily Buzz here: www.tophersbook.com/dailybuzz

Make the Host's Job Easy

One of the other factors in being an incredible guest is being a respectful guest. In other words, respect the host's time and become a servant to their goals first. Don't expect the host to read your book or look over your website. They probably won't. So provide them a list of pre-established questions that you want them to ask you. They will love this. It doesn't mean they will ask all your questions, or in the order that you give them, but it will provide them a start, and they will be grateful for it. When you come up with the questions, don't shy away from the hard ones. If all your questions are about how great your product or service is, the audience starts to feel you are disingenuous and they are watching a poorly produced infomercial. Avoid the self-serving questions, and try to come up with the questions behind the questions like you would if you were the host. In fact, have some zingers in your questions. Ones that otherwise might scare you. In this case they won't because you'll have answers ready to go which redirect the focus to something else. **Remember: Premise, Problem, Solution**. If you just have a premise and a solution, that's a boring show. Put some controversy in the interview, and the host will love you for giving them some tough questions.

For television, always show up with two outfits. Why? Because you don't want to show up wearing the exact colored shirt as the host. If you do, they will love you for bringing a change of clothes so you don't look like Tweedle Dee and Tweedle Dum on air. Of course, the other reason to bring a spare shirt is because you never know who might spill a cup of coffee on you in the greenroom. If you've spilled something on your pants, that can usually be hidden through camera angles, but if you have a big stain on your shirt, that's very hard to disguise. Be prepared. Even if you don't have to use the shirt, when the station sees you arrive prepared, they will be impressed and that will set their minds at ease. How much air time you get depends on two things: How entertaining you are, and whether or not the station's staff and personnel like you. If they don't like you, it doesn't matter how entertaining you are. Your segment is going to get cut short.

Address the host by name more than once—especially for radio. Radio talk show hosts love this because sometimes they are given pre-established questions, along with canned answers from a celebrity. They read the question, the celebrity already has the answer recorded, and the sound engineer splices them together and no matter how much they try, there are still silent gaps, and it just sounds off compared to a real interview. So when you say their name, they like it because they know their audience won't have to wonder if it's a pre-recorded fake interview.

Go wherever the host wants to go as well. There is a rule in improv comedy: whatever happens, go with it. The moment one improv character doesn't want to cooperate with another, it blocks the flow, creates weird energy, and somebody usually ends up looking like a fool. You don't want to be the fool, and you damn sure don't want to make the host look like a fool—unless that's your entertainment objective and you're willing to reap the rewards or suffer the consequences. (The perfect example of this is Jon Stewart's highly Googled interview on "Crossfire"—his blatant disregard for the hosts catapulted his visibility and success with "The Daily Show," but he was already a seasoned professional with a highly successful show of his own.) With improv, no matter what the person who spoke last says, it's your job to utilize that into your skit and then direct it to where you want to go. The same can be said for an interview. If the host asks you a question that you might not want to answer, go with it anyway. Answer it the best you can and then change the focus to where you want it to go. Nobody likes a person who doesn't answer a question. They think you are a slimy politician.

Look Me in the Eyes

Unless you are being interviewed remotely via satellite or video conferencing, don't look at the camera. Look at the host. The moment you look into the camera when a host is interviewing you most, if not all of your credibility will be lost. The unintended effect is that it makes you look uncertain and searching for approval. Ignore the camera. Let the camera be the "fly on the wall" viewpoint for the person watching the interview. As if they are eavesdropping on the conversation. This can sometimes be tricky if it's a multiple camera shoot an their is a camera over the host's shoulder focusing on you. It will be very tempting to look at the camera, but don't do it. It won't look good. Just fixate on the hosts face, make great eye contact, and keep going.

CHAPTER 15

LIGHTS, CAMERA, ACTION!

S peaking in front of—or, more precisely, to—a camera presents some interesting challenges, but worthwhile rewards. Other than live, face-to-face interaction, it's still the best way to connect emotionally with your audience when done correctly. If done poorly, can drive a wedge between you and your audience—maybe even have them tune out and never come back around.

No matter how confident and brilliant they might be speaking in front of a group, most people have the same confidence level of a 14-year-old boy on his first date when they are placed in front of a camera. They become nervous, fidgety, can't put two sentences together, and sweat like a Southern Baptist preacher in July. The reason for this is simple: It's foreign. When anyone is placed into an unfamiliar environment where they have to perform at a high level, most of the time they choke.

As much as I would like to say, "All you have to do is follow these simple tips when in front of a camera and you'll come across approachable and confident every time," the reality is, none of these tips will help you without familiarizing yourself with the cold stare of a camera in front of your face. So this is one of those times where you just need to pull up your big boy or big girl pants and get in front of the lens as much as you can, especially before you have an opportunity to get on TV!

Through the Looking Glass

When speaking to a person in a live, one-on-one setting, you generally look them in the eye. That's where you focus your gaze. So when speaking

in front of a camera, the logical thing would be to look at the lens of the camera. **Don't ever look *at* the lens of the camera.**

Where should you look? *Through* the lens. The simple reason for this is because if you look at the lens you aren't looking at the person watching the video because the viewer's face isn't on the screen, it's about 18 - 24 inches away from the screen.

In order to really connect with the viewer, you want to look through the lens and imagine there is someone on the other side of the camera. By doing this, it changes something inside you. You look at the lens differently. It stops being a cold piece of technology and becomes real. You warm up to it and this, as bizarre as it sounds, it changes how you appear to the viewer. Don't try to figure it out, just try it out, and you'll see what I mean.

When you do this, you want to imagine someone on the other side of the lens that you like. As corny as this sounds, picture someone who warms your heart. It could be the love of your life, one of your kids, a superhero you admire, or your favorite pet. It really doesn't matter. What matters is when you imagine that person on the other side of that lens, it makes you feel good. Not only will this help you to connect emotionally with the viewer, but it will help to alleviate any nervousness you might have speaking to a cold piece of technology.

Show Me Some Cheese

If there is one single tip you can remember when speaking in front of a camera, it would be to smile. We've all heard how the camera adds 10 pounds, but nobody ever talks about why this illusion happens. It's because you are a three-dimensional object, but on video you are flattened into a two-dimensional object. The most notable effect is that people look slightly heavier, but some of the other implications have to do with your smile and your hands.

First, the smile. When speaking to someone in a live setting, you can talk with a normal facial expression and it seems perfectly normal. But on camera, that normal facial expression can come across looking angry. So to prevent that, you want to smile. But not just a normal smile, because it will translate to a smirk on camera. But a really big smile translates to a normal, warm, approachable smile. A good rule of thumb: When speaking to a camera, if your cheeks aren't sore by the time you're done shooting the video, you probably didn't smile enough. Don't take my word for it. Use your smart phone to record you talking about your expertise. Then, watch it back with the volume turned off. Notice how you appear. If you didn't smile during the video, when you watch yourself back, you will even agree that you look like you are ready to punch the camera.

For a side-by-side demonstration of this, watch this video. www.tophersbook.com/smilevid

When you are smiling on camera at the level necessary for it to come across effectively, you will probably feel like you have a big cheesy smile on your face. And you do. But it will look better on camera. If you smile that much on stage or when talking to people one on one, they will probably think you are strange. So remember, big cheesy smiles are for camera talk only (unless you're just cheesy by nature)!

Is There Something in Your Eye?

We've all heard that if you want someone to trust you, look them in the eye. And in most cultures, this is certainly true. But when you are looking someone "in the eye" on camera, you can come across scared or intimidated if you forget to do one thing. And you will most likely forget to do it, because it's one of those things that you never have to think about when speaking in a live environment, but on a camera, for reasons I'm not quite sure of, we just stop doing. That behavior is blinking.

The normal frequency that you blink in your normal life is about 15-20 times per minute. This will slow down to 7-10 times when speaking on camera, even less if you are reading a teleprompter! This simple shift, however, can make you look scared and intimidated. So you want to become conscious of your blinking and do it more frequently than you think you actually should. In time, as you familiarize yourself with a camera and your nerves subside, you'll find yourself blinking at normal rates again. But especially in the beginning phase of your on-camera work, this is one of those things to keep in mind. Don't let that happen. Do it intentionally and make it a habit. You'll be glad you did. Your viewers will be glad you did!

For a side-by-side demonstration of this, watch this video. www.tophersbook.com/blinkvid

Don't Look Down

If you are speaking face to face with someone, and they are constantly looking at your shoes, over your shoulder, or above your head, how would you feel? I'm guessing you would probably start looking around to see what it is that they find so interesting. The same can happen when you are speaking direct to a camera. If your eyes are looking anywhere but at the camera lens, people won't start looking behind them, but will feel like you are emotionally disconnected. And if you look downward on camera, it comes off as dishonesty.

In the real world, looking down typically comes across like you are in thought or getting in touch with your emotions. But in the case of on camera, looking below the plane of your nose often creates the impression you are being dishonest. So if you are going to look off camera, look anywhere but down. But as a general rule, look through the lens and connect with your viewer.

Who is This 'Everyone' You Keep Talking About?

When you are speaking in front of an audience, it's more than acceptable to address the crowd as "everyone" or "everybody." While completely inaccurate from a gender classification, even "you guys" is in most cases is still acceptable. But how strange would it be if you were meeting a friend at your local coffee shop and they walked in, gave you a hug, and said, "Hi everyone, thanks for meeting me for coffee today!"

Those types of phrases should be reserved for live audience presentations where there are multiple people. They are inappropriate to use when speaking to camera. "Hi everybody, thanks for watching this video!" Who is *everybody*? When someone is watching a video, the majority of the time it's just one person watching. This is a subtle, but powerful distinction when trying to connect with the viewer. You already have enough challenges making an emotional connection with someone you can't see, who is watching a two-dimensional version of you, typically on a three-inch screen halfway around the world. Don't make things worse by addressing that one person as *everyone* or *everybody* or *guys*. Instead, act like you are talking to just one person and communicate to them the way you would if they were sitting across a table from you.

Get Grounded

Shifting from side to side is a perfectly natural thing to do when standing on a stage or having a one-on-one conversation. While it can be distracting, it's usually not that big of a deal. But when you are on camera, shifting your body weight from side to side is incredibly distracting. The reason for this is because of the walls to your left and right. The walls are the edge of the video. When you are on stage there are no walls next to you. People can see far beyond your sides so the movement isn't as obvious. But when you have the left and right of the screen typically very close to you, the moment you start shifting it becomes greatly accentuated and is distracting. You want your viewers engaged and connected; not seasick.

So how do you prevent from swaying to the left and right? The more you speak in front of a camera, the less of an issue this will be, but in the beginning you may have to restrict your movement. And the best way to do that is to shoot the video from your waist up. By doing this, you can stand with your legs spread wide. This will prevent you from swaying because you've inhibited your ability to move. Nobody will be the wiser when watching the video. Only you, and whoever is shooting the video will see your silly stance.

The other solution is to shoot your video while sitting down. But beware! If the chair you are sitting on swivels, you'll unconsciously transfer that sway to swiveling in your seat, and that's just as bad. So if you do sit, sit in a chair with four legs that is stationary and without wheels.

PART 3

BEHIND THE DESK

CHAPTER 16

SHOW ME THE MONEY!

Always Get Paid

Peter Montoya is a personal branding guru and author of the bestselling books, "The Personal Branding Phenomenon" and "The Brand Called You." He's travelled all throughout the United States helping the financial services industry develop and create a powerful brand identity. He's been featured in business journals and has been interviewed by every major news show including Wolf Blitzer in the Situation Room on CNN. He's had a remarkably successful career as a professional speaker. Over one of our usual Outback Steakhouse dinners, he shared with me one of his most powerful lessons as a professional speaker that he got at the very beginning of his career. I loved the story so much I thought I would share it with you.

Peter was about 22 years old at the time, wide-eyed and ready to conquer the speaking world, he was sitting in the audience listening to Brian Tracy inspire about 4,000 people in Atlanta. At the end of the event, Peter walked up to Brian and told him he wanted to be a speaker as well, and wondered if he could share with him some advice on succeeding in the profession. Brian stopped what he was doing, looked at Peter straight in the eye, put his hand on his shoulder and said, "Always, always, always, get paid."

That advice sounds so simple most people would overlook how profound it really is. This one piece of advice, if taken to heart can instantly transform you from public to professional speaker. Why don't most people take the advice? Because they haven't explored all the ways they can get paid.

A speaking fee is not the only way to get paid. In fact, in some cases, it may be the least effective way to be paid. But you should ALWAYS get paid. In the beginning, your payment might be a meal. It might be a list of business cards; it might be in the form of a testimonial, or a quote to use with future prospects. But if an organization expects you to show up, give your knowledge, share your stories, and give them everything you have to inspire their hearts and help them to improve, and they won't let you so much as collect business cards, or sell a book, then the answer is simple. Tell them "No thank you."

There are only two reasons why you would want to ever speak with a condition that you get nothing in return. First, you have some new material that you need to try out on a test-crowd, and you don't want to experiment with a paid audience. Second, you are speaking for a charity that is dear to your heart and it's your part of tithing and contribution. Both of these reasons are very valid and trump even Brian Tracy's advice.

So if you are going to get compensated for your speaking efforts, and you MUST do this from the very beginning of your career, the next most logical step would be to secure a contract with the individual or organization that is hiring you to speak. Even if you are getting paid with a meal or the right to sell a product, have a speaking contract signed by yourself and the party that is booking you. It eliminates confusion; it creates clarity for both parties on their roles and responsibilities and, perhaps just as important, it tells them you are a professional.

How much should you expect to pay for a speakers contract to be drafted? I paid nearly $3,000 for my attorneys to write a generic contract that I use for all of my speaking arrangements.

If $3,000 seems like a great deal of money to spend on a contract, then allow me to share with you just one of the returns it has helped me to secure.

I was hired several years back by a seminar company to co-train with another speaker. It was a two-week training program for people wanting to become professional speakers. In my contract, it clearly stated that payment needed to be made in full before I got on the plane. With less than three days before the event, and countless phone calls to the company, I still hadn't been paid. I informed them that my contract states I must be paid before I board the plane or I won't get on the plane. They asked me if I would be willing to be paid when I arrived. A simple request, but one that all too often leads in the company saying, "We haven't got the checkbook with us, we'll mail it to you later." This inevitably leads to me or my staff turning into a collections agency. We then waste time and money trying to get paid. And in some cases, we end up never being paid.

So I calmly told them no, and said the contract was clear, I needed my funds. They scrambled to get me my money, and two hours before the flight took off, the funds showed up in my account. When I landed in the UK, I was picked up by one of the company's staff and informed that I would be staying at a house a few miles away from the venue with some of the crew for the event. My contract clearly states that I must be provided hotel accommodations at the venue and the hotel must have gym facilities, dry cleaning, and high-speed Internet access. For me to stay at a house with volunteer staff for the event would mean I would be forced to have confidential business conversations with my staff back in Tampa in the presence of ears that shouldn't hear those conversations. It would mean I would need to be driven to a gym for my daily workouts, wasting precious minutes in driving to and from the gym. Overall, it meant inconvenience. I calmly told the driver to take me to the hotel because my contract was clear. He called his boss, and he said they couldn't do that. I told the driver, quite calmly, to take me back to the airport. Now remember, if I would have flown to the event without being paid in advance, I would have no power to negotiate or enforce my contract, but I had been paid in full, they were in breach of contract, and I could quite easily get back on the next flight, head home, and still keep their money. Knowing that I was holding true to the signed contracts, they were forced to comply with our previously agreed-upon conditions and they booked me a hotel room. No drama, no arguing, no problem.

Was my contract worth the $3,000 I paid? You bet! It has paid for itself hundreds of times over. As your mentor, take my advice. Get a contract immediately. If you have local legal contacts, a friend in the business, or know of a reputable firm that doesn't charge as much, you might pay as little as a few hundred dollars for such a contract. Regardless, it is worth the investment.

Would you like to see a sample of my contract? I'd be happy to offer it for you today for simply filling out a small survey. By doing so, you'll help me to better understand the needs of my customers, and in turn, you'll save yourself thousands of dollars on having to pay an attorney to draft a speaker's contract. Click the link below to get started, and in less than 15 minutes, you'll have a copy of the exact speaker's contract that I paid $3,000 to have written, and I still use to this day.

Click here to take the survey and grab the contract: www.tophersbook.com/contract

NOTE: This contract in no way should replace your goal to seek legal counsel. Take this contract to them, have them review it, and make any changes necessary based upon the state or country that you live in. You should only have to pay for an hour of their consulting, saving you a great deal of money.

Critical Error #1—Stop Thinking You Are Kevin Costner!

Most would-be speakers have a "Field of Dreams" mentality. In other words, just like in the movie, they think… "If you build it, they will come." And nothing could be further from the truth.

So many struggling speakers think that if they make a website that talks about their seminar, and/or a one page flyer, then people will be signing up left and right to do business with them. They go out, book a huge venue that can accommodate hundreds, maybe even thousands of people, and after the contracts are signed, they discover just how hard it can be sometimes to put people in a room. Inevitably, they have to cancel the event for lack of sales, or keep the venue, conduct the seminar, and have a small group of people sit in a conference room 100 times too big for the audience in attendance (which damages their credibility and makes them look pretty stupid). Either way, the struggling speaker still owes the hotel tens of thousands of dollars and for many, this mistake creates an unrecoverable error in their business.

Helpful Hint #1—Start Thinking You Are the Karate Kid!

Instead of booking the venue months in advance with the expectation of booking hundreds or thousands of people, wait until the last possible moment. Ralph Macchio, in "The Karate Kid" wanted to learn the crane technique, but Mr. Miyagi new he wasn't ready... The Karate Kid heeded his advice and did not use the technique until the last possible moment... he also knew that you shouldn't fight unless it's absolutely necessary. When booking your venue for your event, this should be your goal as well. If you wait until the last possible moment to book your venue (ideally less than two weeks from the event), you will get the venue for far less money. The same room that you wanted three months in advance will now be 50-90% less than you would have paid if you signed the contracts up front.

There is an inherent risk involved when advertising a venue that you haven't yet signed a contract for: The venue may not be available, but assuming you are conducting your event in a major city, there is one safe rule you can always rely on: There is always another venue available somewhere. (Except during the holidays which you should never book an event during anyway.) Yes, you will have to send a notice to all those who have signed up letting them know of the change in venue, but that inconvenience is a small price to pay to minimize your risk and keep your profit margins as high as possible.

Helpful Hint #2—The Key to Big Money... Think Small!

If your circumstances don't allow for a last-minute booking, then make sure you book a venue that has scalable rooms, and rent the smallest room available. Many hotels, for example, have conference rooms that can accommodate as few as 10 people and as many as 5,000. Instead of booking the 5,000-person venue, ask yourself, "If my marketing bombed, and my sales stunk, what would my worst case scenario of attendance be for my course?" Book that sized venue. Now if you are a motivational speaker, you're probably thinking, "But that's negative thinking! I've got my vision board, a clearly defined goal, and passion!" Well, good for you. Try paying your bills with your positive mental attitude, your dream board, or your clearly defined goals. Positive mental attitude is a great thing, but if not tempered with smart business acumen and a conservative business strategy, your positive mental attitude most likely will just keep a smile on your face as you fail.

You also might be thinking, "But what if I sell too many tickets and I have too many people show up for my small venue?" Trust me, this is just the kind of problem you want to have as a professional speaker! It's also why you book a venue that can increase, as your demands require. Here's a hypothetical example:

Your local hotel will charge you $1,500 per day for a venue that holds 500 delegates.

You book a room that can only accommodate 25 delegates for $150 per day.

One month out from your event, you have sold 40 or more tickets… you contact the hotel and ask them if they have a room than can accommodate 75 people. They say yes, and you ask them if it's available. It is, and they agree to give it to you for $200 per day because with less than a month to go, it's unlikely they will be able to rent it out anyway. You apply your $150 per day for the smaller room toward the bigger room and you only pay $50 per day more. (Most of the time, if you have sufficient rapport established with the banquet manager, they'll just give you the upgrade for free.) Then, you keep selling and you have more than 90 people enrolled with less than a week to go. You call the banquet manager, tell them your situation, and ask them if they have a room that can hold 125-150 people. They say yes, you ask if it's available and they say yes again. You ask them kindly, "Would you mind just moving us to that room? I think we are going to have more people than we expected." Most likely, they will just give it to you that close to the event, but even if they do charge you, it will still be significantly less than had you booked it in advance.

I realize that the hypothetical above takes into consideration many conditions like the rooms not being used, but if you find a large enough venue, this scenario is far more common than you might think.

If, however, the venue does not have the available conference space, then it's simply a matter of contacting another venue at the last minute and finding one that can accommodate your needs. The best part of all is they will give you the space for a bargain because nobody will likely book it at the last minute. So you happily walk away from the old venue and don't even think about asking for your money back. The money you walk away from at the old venue combined with the great discount you receive from the new venue is still less money than the amount you would have spent reserving the new venue many months ago. This type of moving from venue to venue is okay because it's in the contract and they plan for situations just like this. Believe me, if you've put down $1,000 to reserve a venue and then you cancel the event and you don't ask for the money back, they will be happy because they just received $1,000 without having to staff their venue or even turn on the lights.

Helpful Hint #3—Find a Mentor

As an entrepreneur turning into a professional speaker, there is one humbling truth that, if accepted, will save you from wasting untold amounts of time, substantial money, and unnecessary frustration. Here is the truth: You aren't unique, and your message isn't unique. (clearly I'm not a motivational speaker.) The problems and challenges that you are or will be facing have already been met with and conquered by someone else.

The way I see it, you have two options.

Option #1: Solve those problems and challenges on your own. If you choose this route, it will be very costly. Many have gone this route only to go bankrupt before they could get their message out to the people who really needed it.

Option #2: Find someone in the business who is willing to share with you the solutions to those problems and challenges. By having someone like this in your corner, you are far more likely to achieve that lifestyle that so few speakers ever obtain.

You deserve an amazing life. Your message deserves to be heard by more people than you are currently reaching. Those people are waiting to discover who you are, and that life is waiting for you recognize it.

CHAPTER 17

THE ULTIMATE FAIR-WEATHERED FRIEND

Travel down this hypothetical path: You are trying to sell your products or services at a public speaking event. You know the success of your sales will determine what your quality of life is like in your company for the next few months. After your pitch, you politely wait in the back of the room to make your sales. But people don't seem to be rushing to the back of the room to sign up for the offer you presented from stage; you can't afford to lose one single sale. So for the few who do come back, you want to maximize every opportunity. You are collecting payment and get to the part where you need to explain your refund policy. You know that if you point out the refund policy, they might say, "No thank you." You also realize if you don't make a big deal about the refund policy, the excitement of the purchase will overshadow their need to read the fine print and you'll make the sale. Plus, you are in a hurry because there are a few other potential sales you can get to before they walk out the door. What will you do?

This is not just a typical scenario. In the beginning of your business, it's most likely the ONLY scenario you will encounter when conducting your introductory events.

In most cases, desperation overtakes your certainty and you cave into just making the sale, so you skim over the refund policy or don't even talk about it at all. It feels good in the short term, but as you approach the date of the time you must deliver your services to the client, this split-second decision will cause you countless amounts of heartache, stress, and anxiety. It is, categorically, not worth the short-term success in the beginning. This type of action spells disaster in the speaking business. Remember this motto:

Short-Term Desperation = Long-Term Failure

This is almost impossible to conceive, but the person who is signing up for your offer and worried about whether or not they will have time to use the very services they are buying from you, and wants a way out, and is concerned about your refund policy, and wants you to modify your refund policy to make them feel more comfortable will drop out and demand that you give them their money back anyway.

So it's rarely, if ever worth getting the sale with these customers. Remember this: It's better to have 10 committed customers than 50 questionable customers. How can you ensure you have committed customers? Make sure your refund policies are crystal clear and have them sign the registration form, contract, or on-boarding document that indicates what those policies are. Even better, read them out to them.

It is natural for someone to try to back out at the last minute. Many people get scared at the thought of changing their life for the better so they will try to cancel. It is your job to make this as difficult as possible. It may mean being the 'bad guy' in the beginning in order to get them to attend. If you fail to keep them enrolled, then depending upon your refund policy, you may be forced to return a great deal of money, but ultimately, the depressing part is that you have failed to inspire someone to make changes in their life, or their profession, which will solve some big problems for them and make their life or business more joyful.

You Are in the Business of Helping People

Examine the above sentence. Of the two parts, which is more important, that you are in business or that you help people? The answer to that question is simple to identify, but very hard to live by. The answer is that you are in business, and as such, you need to run it like a business.

If you were to buy a ticket to a musical or play, and then not be able to attend at the last minute, would you call the theatre and ask for a refund? If you were to buy a ticket to the World Cup and then not be able to attend, would you call the stadium and ask them for a refund? If you bought a season pass to a theme park and then never ended up going, would you call them up at the end of the year and ask for your money back? The answer to all of these questions, of course, is no. Although I'm sure there are a few people out there who would try, the majority of the public would realize that that you made a business transaction and whether you attend or not is not the responsibility of the party who sold you the ticket. However, in the seminar business, for some reason people think they are entitled to receive their money back if they buy a ticket and then change their mind at the last minute.

You are running a business. You need to forecast, you need to budget, you need to make good on the commitments you've made to paying your staff and your other financial obligations. You need to recoup the money you have invested in advertising and administration. The money to pay for those commitments, and the accuracy of your budgeting and forecasting, is dependent upon the reliability of your sales. It is your responsibility to ensure that you've done everything possible to make those sales as secure as possible.

As you read this chapter, if you haven't yet experienced selling tickets to your first seminar, you are probably thinking I am paranoid and that there is no way a person would have the nerve to demand their money back at the last minute. So this is where it's time for you to do your due diligence. Reach out to some professional speakers (make sure they are professional, not amateur speakers), and ask them if I am accurate or not. I can promise you they will all share the same experience. You would be shocked at how many people have last-minute emergencies, deaths in the family, and terrible illnesses that prevent them from going to the program. Of course, 99% of those excuses are just lies that they are telling you to get you to feel sympathetic to their cause, cave in, and give them their money back.

By having a clearly established refund policy which is fair to both you and the customer, customers may still get angry, but when you do not give them all their money back, it will at least give you a strong foundation to fall back on.

Here are some key points to include in your refund policy:

- **Avoid Percentages, Include Actual Amounts.**
  Some time ago, I had a customer who enrolled into one of my seminars ask for his money back as the seminar was approaching. My refund policy at the time was very clear: 25% of the tuition was non-refundable. The challenge was that I had given him a student discount from the tuition, so in his mind the tuition for the program was what he paid, not what the actual tuition was. When his finances got tight and he was faced with the reality of how expensive the seminar would be with hotel, airfare, and meals, he decided to pull out at the last minute and he wanted his money back. I happily honored my refund policy and gave him all of his money back, less 25% of the tuition. He wanted all of his money back less 25% of what he paid. When he found out he would be receiving a lesser amount, it upset him and he got so outraged he started demanding 100% of his money back. What he failed to understand is that even though he received a student discount, the costs incurred to my company to have him attend were just as high as someone who isn't a student. The student discount only did one thing, cut into my profit. But the commission for my sales rep was still the same, including the labor costs incurred for my administrative staff to create a file for him, reserve a seat for him, and maintain customer service.

  To prevent this confusion from happening with your customers, I recommend stating how much in financial terms a cancellation will cost the customer. Instead of stating, "…25% of the course fee is non-refundable," have your policy read, "… there is a $_____ non-refundable deposit." This will avoid any confusion later on should a similar situation occur.

- **Get Their Agreement, Not Just a Signature.**

  With smart phones and laptop computers, you can very easily record a verbal agreement with little to no effort. Much like the operator may transfer you to a third party confirmation after you purchase something over the phone, you should also have a record of your customer agreeing to the terms and conditions of your policies. Remember, this still won't prevent them from demanding all of their money back; it will simply strengthen your position when you enforce your policies. I've included a script for you to use below when recording their agreement to your terms and conditions:

  "Thank you for your purchase. Now before we finalize everything and process the charge, I'm going to record the terms and conditions for your file and our records. [Start Recording] Can you please state your full name and address? Thank you, our terms and conditions are as follows: [Read your terms & conditions.] Are you agreeable to the terms and conditions I just read to you? [wait for response] Very well, everything is set and you are officially enrolled, congratulations!"

  Remember, if they are not agreeable to your terms and conditions, they are a high-risk client and not worth the sale. It's better to walk away from the sale upfront than to have to deal with an irate customer in the end.

CHAPTER 18

FINDING A PROMOTER

Unless you are a celebrity, professional athlete, or have been fortunate enough to publish a best-selling book, finding a company to promote your seminars is a bit like a unicorn. I can't prove they don't exist, but to date, I haven't seen one.

In the beginning of your speaking career, you will most likely be the speaker, the promoter, the sales person, the secretary, and the janitor all in one. Consider it the part of your career where you pay your dues. If you do this correctly, though, at some point, promoters will find you and want to do business with you. How long will that be? When I started Topher Morrison, Inc., it took me nearly six years to find someone reliable to promote me, and before finding them, I went through several other less reliable and some rather unscrupulous promoters before I finally found some trustworthy companies. If you concentrate on what I'm about to share with you in this chapter, you will shave several years off your otherwise frustrating quest to find a promoter.

Dent Global is one of the most successful training companies in the UK. They have a very loyal customer base for one main reason: They consistently book the most dynamic and informative speakers. If you receive an email from Dent Global promoting a seminar, there is one thing you can bet on: The seminar will be great, and it will be worth the investment. They have purposefully steered far away from the typical, multi-speaker events that have one sole purpose—selling you additional products. This isn't to say that they don't have multi-speaker events. They do, and they are the best in the industry. But they look for speakers that can do more than just sell a product to an audience. Speakers who want to be promoted by Dent Global are always approaching Daniel Priestly, the CEO. He says he looks for five specific factors when booking a speaker:

1. **Clarity in the market**

   Does the speaker have a reputation? Are they known for something? When people hear their name, do they immediately associate a brand, topic, or specialty to that person?

2. **Credibility in the market**

   It's one thing for people to know an individual, but do they respect them as well? Is that reputation that they have a good one? One where people think highly enough of the individual that they would be willing to take time out of their day to receive some advice from that person?

3. **Variability**

   Are they more than a one-trick-pony? Do they have a vast enough knowledge about their specialty that they could come back several times over, but not repeat themselves, and consistently provide new, current, relevant information to the audience?

4. **Visibility**

   Are they well-known? Do they attract a crowd? Are they famous enough that people want to talk about them? Does their reputation precede them and create a buzz?

5. **Collaborative Spirit**

   Are they willing and able to help promote the event to their customer base in such a way that their die-hard fans will show up and then become a part of Dent's growing fan base?

CHAPTER 19

YOU EXPECT ME TO PAY HOW MUCH?

Arguably, one of the biggest determinants in the success of your business, as in all businesses, will be your price points. In the world of seminars, your goal as an entrepreneur is to get the maximum amount of profit possible without taking advantage of your clients, yet charge as little as possible without turning your business into a charity. So how do you know what you should charge? Well, there are two ways:

1. Pull the prices out of your butt. That's what most speakers do.
2. Create a formula. This requires a bit more thought, but, in the end, is far less painful.

Here's how I justify my prices: I've accepted long ago that seminars are about helping a little group of people a lot, and a lot of people a little.

Despite the typical self-help nonsense some seminar companies hype, no one ever produces a 90-plus percentage rate of successful clients. In a seminar of 1,000 people attending an Internet marketing course, one or two people will actually go out and make money at it. In a seminar of 100 people attending any vocational certification course, one or two people will actually go out and make money at it. In a seminar of only 20 people learning how to become day traders, only one or two people will actually go out and make money at it. Are you seeing a pattern?

No matter how many are in attendance, there's typically only a handful that will walk away with a life-altering result. And that's perfectly okay. The key for me has always been to ask myself what I could charge, that if the client only received the minor change in their life they would receive their money's worth. The people who are blessed to have a life-altering experience get 100 times the value they paid.

For example, at my Legacy event, which trained people to become professional speakers, I know that regardless of what I charged, the majority of the people who attended would never make it as a successful professional speaker no matter how committed I was to seeing them succeed. This is the main reason I no longer offer the course. While some never want to be a professional speaker in the first place, others will discover that it's harder work than anticipated and they aren't willing to do what they need to do to succeed. So I ask myself what would it be worth for someone to attend a course for two weeks and develop some speaking skills for life, and be mentored for one year, which, if nothing else, creates powerful friendships and holds them accountable for their actions? I felt that just receiving those two benefits is worth the tuition of $20,000. If I were to charge the value for life-altering transformation and becoming a successful professional speaker who on average earns $10,000 per speaking engagement and gets to travel the world, see amazing sights, and go to bed at night knowing their income is a direct reflection of how many lives they have touched, the value for that would easily be worth $200,000. That's what universities do. Their tuition reflects the value for succeeding as a result of your degree and changing your life massively. But how many people have you met who never end up working in the field of their chosen degree? If I were to charge $200,000 for Legacy, the majority of my customers would probably feel like they didn't receive the value I charged, and they would be right. But by keeping my pricing on the lower end scale of $20,000, I can be certain that the people in attendance would be getting their value. Think about it this way, the worst-case scenario for a Legacy graduate would be that they pay $20,000 to discover that they don't want to be a speaker. If they were to get that lesson on their own, they would most likely be in debt over $100,000 and in misery for well over a year before they finally admitted it. The way I see it, a $20,000 investment to get the worst-case scenario saves them about $80,000 and year of frustration.

This is only the first part of my equation however. If you don't take into consideration the financial costs you have to incur for each person in attendance, you still may be setting a price so low you leave no room for profit.

Consider these factors when establishing your pricing:

1. What are my total labor costs in between each seminar I am selling? Your sales must not only cover the expense of the event, but the expenses of your business that you need to run in between events.

2. What is my total overhead for office administration such as office lease, office supplies, phone bills, utilities, insurance, certification boards and membership dues, training programs for your staff or yourself, production of the training manuals, gift packages for people who sign up, taxes, and marketing costs like pay-per-click, printing of brochures, and bulk mail postage?

3. Am I getting a speaking fee? As the CEO and professional speaker for your business, you have your regular salary for running the business, but you should also be receiving a speaker's fee for your time on stage.

4. How much does it cost for each chair in my event? This will be a best guess, but when planning your event, if you expect on having 20 people in attendance and your venue is $500 per day, it will cost you $25 per seat.

5. How much does it cost per person for refreshments at my event? This is always one of the greatest shock factors in the business for beginning speakers. Conference rooms in a hotel charge prices for coffee, tea, and snacks that are way beyond the extortion fees the mob charges to "protect" a business in their neighborhood. Would you like a vegetable tray at your events? It can cost upwards of $15 per person for carrot sticks and broccoli! How about some coffee? I've paid more than $60 in some places for a carafe of coffee! Be very aware of these prices before you negotiate your room rates. Often hotels will give you a very low conference room rate, but neglect to tell you that they are going to stick it to you when you want to get a cup of coffee for your customers.

6. Unforeseen expenses? Trust me, at every seminar there is an unforeseen expense. You will forget something at home, it will be too far to go back to get it, and you'll have to buy a replacement immediately. This happens with speaker cables, batteries, paper, power supply cords, ties, shirts, and shoes. Did you request a flip chart at the time of booking? No? Did they mention that they charge $50 per day to rent a flip chart that only costs $25 at Office Depot but there isn't one nearby? Now you want a stage for your event? That will be another $300 per day. Room doesn't look like you wanted it to? The hotel has

a clause in their contract that any rework on the setup of the room is an additional 10% fee. You name it; I've had to pay for it. And you will, too. So budget for it. I add an additional $75 per day in unexpected expenses for every event day, and I'm probably underestimating those costs.

7. Any special event costs? Celebration party at the end? Special guest speakers you are bringing in? All of these special events can be quite expensive and if you don't factor those into your budget, your profit margins significantly decrease.

All in all, it's far more expensive to run an event than people think. I always have to laugh when someone walks up during a break and says something to the effect of, "Hey, you made out all right on this event—$5,000 per head, 30 people in the room; you walked away with $150,000. Not bad for seven days work." Seven days' work? They failed to consider the four months of expenses it took to promote the event.

Take all of the expenses that you calculate above, divide it by the number of attendees you anticipate having, and then subtract that from the ticket price of the event you want to charge. The difference will be your anticipated profit. Assuming the ticket price is higher than the expenses per head, ask yourself one very important question: Is the anticipated profit worth the time, effort, and energy you am going to have to incur in order to pull this event off? If the answer is no, then go back to the drawing board. If the answer is yes, ask yourself the exact same question after the event to make sure you still agree with your original answer and add an additional question: Did the event actually turn any profit?

One last, but very important distinction—profit for the event CAN NOT include money you made for future seminar sales. Those monies need to be calculated for that seminar in the future. If you are including seminar sales for future events in your calculation for the profit of your current event, you are essentially "robbing from Peter to pay Paul." In the world of finance, that's known as a Ponzi scheme. No matter how good you are at using future sales to pay for current expenses, it will eventually catch up with you. Just ask Bernie Madoff.

Did this chapter leave you feeling a bit overwhelmed? I've created a "plug & play" system for you to use that allows you to calculate the true profit margins of an event that will save you time and money. If you would like, it's my gift to you as a way of saying "thank you" for purchasing my book. Just click here and take it for free. www.tophersbook.com/calculator

CHAPTER 20

ONE PAGE, MANY REQUESTS

This chapter is dedicated to the most important tool a keynote speaker has in his or her arsenal. If your style of speaking is more seminar- or workshop-based, you will still want to utilize this tool. Why? Because even as a seminar or workshop facilitator, you will be given the opportunity to present keynotes occasionally. Whether or not you get booked for these keynotes is entirely up to how you leverage this tool. What is the tool I'm referring to? The One-Page.

A one-page (also referred to as a one-sheet) is a term common to keynote speakers and speaker's bureaus. If you try to have a speaker's bureau represent you, the two things they will ask you for are a demonstration video (typically, a link to an online video) showcasing your talents, and a one-page. We will address the demonstration video in a future chapter, but for now, the more important and urgent tool is the one-page. Why? Because if someone is inviting you to be a keynote speaker, you can assume they have already seen your speaking talents and now the one-page is just the formality they need to present the idea to a board, which will make the final decision for your presentation. The majority of my keynotes are booked with just a one-page and not a demo video. In these cases, the one person on the panel who has seen me speak becomes an advocate for me, and the panel or board who cuts the check trusts their judgment.

A one-page is exactly what it sounds like. It's ONE PAGE! Not two or three. Only one single page that covers four areas:

1. Your brief bio
2. What they will learn in the keynote
3. Testimonial quotes from happy customers
4. Booking information (who to contact)

Your Brief Bio

Your bio should be approximately one-quarter of the page, or about 200 words in length. While there are many theories out there as to what should or should not be in a bio, there is one rule every successful keynote speaker follows: To illustrate this one rule, I've provided my bio below with 2 versions. Read the two bios below. They are identical with one exception. Notice how you feel about me after each bio and notice the differences.

Bio Version 1:

I was recently accepted onto the University of Tampa's Board of Fellows and provide mentorship to students attending the Sykes College of Business and the Lowth Entrepreneurship Center.

In contrast to most professional development experts, my shockingly honest and irresistibly down-to-earth approach is surprisingly infectious.

My personality and straightforward manner are endearing to audiences who are tired of fleeting success in self-help sinkholes. I'm not afraid to tell it like it is and shatter the myth of achieving ideal perfection. Instead, I reach people across all aspects of an organization and share with them actionable skills and tools to make change that lasts and create desired results in short order.

I'm internationally recognized for my columns on business development, keynotes, and leadership training. I'm the author of the best-selling book, "Stop Chasing Perfection and SETTLE FOR EXCELLENCE," which I'm describing as the self-help book for people who are tired of self-help books and "Collaboration Economy," the go-to handbook for small business owners.

Bio Version 2:

As a recent member of the University of Tampa's Board of Fellows. Topher Morrison provides mentorship to students attending the Sykes College of Business and the Lowth Entrepreneurship Center.

In contrast to most personal development experts, Topher's shockingly honest and irresistibly down-to-earth approach is surprisingly infectious. His personality and straightforward manner are endearing to audiences who are tired of fleeting success in self-help sinkholes. He is not afraid to tell it like it is and shatter the myth of achieving ideal perfection. Instead, Topher reaches people across all aspects of an organization and shares with them actionable skills and tools to make change that lasts and create desired results in short order.

Topher is internationally recognized for his columns on business development, keynotes, and leadership training. He is the author of the best-selling books, "Stop Chasing Perfection and SETTLE FOR EXCELLENCE" and "Collaboration Economy," the go-to handbook for small business owners.

Chances are, the first version turned you off. Why? Because it was written in first person, and while first person text can be an effective tool in website sales, it comes across as strange and arrogant in a bio. Always make sure your bio is written in third person. Third person bios create a more objective impression in the readers mind.

What They Will Learn in the Keynote

This is usually best if written in one sentence or a brief paragraph leading into a bulleted list of what benefits they will receive after hearing you speak. The important thing to remember is BENEFITS… do not tell them the features! I've provided an excerpt of my one-page in two different versions. Notice which one inspires you to want to learn more.

What You Will Learn Version 1

When Topher delivers his keynote, "Success in the Collaboration Age," your audience will not just be entertained and inspired, they will learn:

- How to become a KPI
- How to create a "Who" focused business
- How to apply the "Name, Same, Claim to Fame" technique to their pitch

What You Will Learn Version 2

When Topher delivers his keynote, "Success in the Collaboration Age," your audience will not just be entertained and inspired, they will learn how to:

- Attract business opportunities without having to chase down sales
- Create an irresistible brand identity

- Develop a powerful 30-second pitch that leaves people asking for your business card.

Chances are, the first version was not as intriguing as the second. Always make sure your bulleted points create a specific image in the reader's mind that you have determined in advance. For example, "get motivated" is so ambiguous we don't know how someone will interpret that. For some, "get motivated" conjures up images of their convention participants jumping up and down on chairs chanting, 'I can do it!' whereas others hear the same phrase and think about going for a run. It's the same phrase, but each listener has a totally different image in their mind. But to say, "Develop a powerful 30-second pitch that leaves people asking for your business card" is a specific image that will be mostly the same for everyone.

Booking Information (who to contact)

The one-page should have a pre-designated area where you can insert speaker's bureau information, or your own individual contact information. It's important to remember that you should have as many contact options available in this section—not just a phone number. You will need:

- Phone
- Email address
- Website address
- Website addresses for sample videos
- Mailing address

If the one-page you are creating is online or digital, the .pdf document should have the email and website links hyperlinked so they can simply click on them to contact you.

If you would like to see a sample one-page, you can download mine here: www.tophersbook.com/onepage

CHAPTER 21

RISK MINIMIZERS

The more your popularity as a speaker grows, the more you will be contacted by promoters asking you to speak at their events. The offer will be very typical. They will expect you to pay for all of your expenses—airfare, hotel, food, shipping of product, etc. They will promote the event and be responsible for selling the tickets. The exchange? They will want 50% of all of your sales. You might think that type of a commission is a bit high at first, but the promoter will convince you this is fair because they are absorbing all the risk for the event. This way of thinking, of course, is flawed and incredibly one-sided. These types of speaking arrangements are my least favored and I never accept the offer as they present it. Here's why:

In this type of an environment, there are too many factors outside of your control. These factors have a direct impact on your ability to sell from the stage, and rarely are those factors positive. When the promoter claims that they are assuming all the risk, they have overlooked the risks you will be taking with regard to who the other speakers will be, how well they engage the audience before you get up there, how much money they extract from the audience before you have a chance to sell, how effective or ineffective your sales will be if the attendance is low, and too many other risks to predict in this chapter. Here are some case histories of a few of the problems mentioned above.

Case Study #1

I was asked to speak for a multi-speaker event over a period of four days. There were actually two seminars running simultaneously in two different cities, so I would have to speak at one event, get on a train, and head to a neighboring country, speak there for two days, get back on the train to the original location, and speak one final time. The promoter said there would be a minimum of 300 + paid attendees at this event. When I arrived at the venue the morning of my keynote, this is what I saw:

I flew halfway across the globe to speak for 18 people! If I were to do a 50% split with the promoter for this event, my 50% split based on statistical sales averages wouldn't have even covered my flight. This is why agreeing to do a 50% split with the promoter is ALWAYS a bad idea.

Case Study #2

The owner of a mortgage company went to a motivational seminar. Loving the information so much, he decided he would be a motivational speaker, too. He decides the best route would be to get four key speakers in addition to himself and then promote the event to his network of real estate agents and past customers. They rented a huge venue (first big mistake) and began the promotion. He was a good friend of my personal assistant at the time, so as a personal favor to her, I agreed to speak for his event. He was filled with optimism and great expectations of attracting 400 people. The end result? He had about 60. If I had forecasted my business' needs based upon the anticipated sales I would make on a 400-person audience, I would have created an unrealistic budget, and in the beginning of my business, I did that a lot. I've already mentioned that this is the first huge factor that is outside your control as a speaker, so there's really no need to repeat this lesson. The reason I'm sharing this case study with you is because it gets even worse: I was scheduled to be the final speaker for the day and would have been able to make a reasonable sale with only 60 people in the audience. Unfortunately, the speaker before me was so arrogant in his alleged success, so obnoxious in his sales pitch, and so scattered in his message that by the time he finished his grandstanding, he had dwindled the audience down to only 13 people!

When you agree to speak at a multi-speaker event, even if the promoters do an excellent job getting an audience to show, there's no way you can control how many people will actually stick around to hear your presentation. If the speakers before you are terrible, you will suffer the result. If the promoters don't do their job and get the correct number of people in the room, then the problem is compounded. So how do you solve these problems?

Solution #1

When a promoter is promising big numbers, then they should be willing to back that up. I never agree to a 50/50 split unless they agree to a minimum number of people in the audience. I specify in the payment terms of my contract that if they do not have a minimum number of people sitting in the audience at the time of my presentation, I receive the first $10,000 in sales to cover my expenses. Only after the first $10,000 in sales will we begin to do a commission split. If they are unwilling to agree to this, I simply decline the event. Remember, this is a guarantee of how many people are sitting in the audience, not how many booked or even showed up that day. If they meet their minimum number of attendees, the speaker before me turns the audience away, and I'm left with less than my agreed upon minimum, the $10,000 clause is in effect.

Solution #2

Be selective about which events you speak at, and more importantly, which speakers are going to be sharing the stage with you. I have a list of speakers who have historically turned off audiences by their arrogance, or have terrible reputations for how they provide customer service, and I'm not willing to share the stage with them. I state upfront that if they wish to book any of the speakers on my list, I am not interested in speaking at their event. You must stay on top of this as well. I recently agreed to speak at an event, I didn't follow their marketing efforts, and they ended up booking someone after I agreed to attend, and the person they booked was on my list. I didn't discover this until I arrived at the venue, so it was too late to back out and I didn't feel right not going on stage. That wouldn't have been fair to the audience that came to see me speak. I did, however, send the promoters an email requesting that they immediately remove my name and photograph from all of their seminar marketing. The seminar was already over, but

I didn't care, I didn't want my name associated with the other speaker on any search engines. In this situation, it was an honest mistake, but never underestimate what a promoter will do when they are desperate to get some speakers for their event.

At the end of the day, remember this, the more desperate you are for a speaking event, and the more you are willing to allow the promoter to set all the rules, the lower your ability to be in control of your success. Be willing to walk away from less than ideal situations. You'll be glad you did.

CHAPTER 22

YOU'RE BOUND TO HAVE SOME BUMPS

L et's face it. Even as a speaker who inspires audiences wherever you go, you are bound to have some bumps along your journey. Ups and downs are a part of nature and they are just as present in the speaking business as they are in any other industry.

How can you maximize the ups and minimize the downs? In this chapter, I've compiled a list of specific things I ignored, neglected, or simply didn't acknowledge at the time that led to my company losing money and, in one large case, nearly cost me my enterprise. I'm sharing these with you now for two reasons. Firstly, so that when they do inevitably happen to you, you will realize you are not alone and it doesn't mean you are a failure. Second, by reading these now, you'll be able to immediately course correct and get back on track if something similar surfaces for you.

Warning Sign #1

The first sign that something isn't right is when people ask you how things are going, you say, "Great!" but cannot offer any specific areas where it actually is going great. Positive mental attitudes are wonderful, but when those attitudes are serving as denial mechanisms, they can be very dangerous. Pay attention to this! If things aren't going great in your business, don't tell people they are. If you do, then you are just another one of those inauthentic people in self–help who are lying to themselves and their friends. I'm not saying complain about your life either. Here's a recent example of how I've handled this situation in my life. In 2009 I officially retired from the business of self-help seminars—a profession that served me very well and provided me a wonderful life for 20 years. As I was winding down that part of my business, I had a plan to ramp up my corporate keynotes and speaker training seminars. The winding down went faster than the starting up and I experienced a few months where I needed to personally loan my company money to cover the monthly expenses. When people would ask me how things were going, I would usually respond with something like, "Well, it's been an interesting few months. I've been learning some great lessons about transitions in business and I think I'm finally seeing the light at the end of the tunnel." To me, this seemed authentic, but also positive. I never sat down on the couch and complained about the economy or whined that my business wasn't reaching the revenue projections I had hoped for. I simply focused on the lessons, stated them, and moved on. The surprising thing for me was when I did this, the person who I was speaking with echoed similar sentiment on how their business had recently been slow—sometimes right after they had told me everything was going great.

Warning Sign #2

If you ever have to wonder if your credit card will get approved when taking a client out to lunch, your spending is out of hand, or your financial accountability is lacking.

You should never have to wonder if a card is going to get approved or not. If you do, it's time to curb your spending habits and realize, whether it seems like it or not, you are in crisis mode and you MUST stop the bleeding.

Warning Sign #3

You are buying consumable products for your business on credit. Food, fuel for your car, the utilities, and entertainment. All of these things should be paid for with cash or a debit card. If you are purchasing these items on credit, then you are moving backward financially every month. It makes no sense to keep paying interest long after the thing you purchased is gone. I don't mind buying items for my business on credit, but that's only if the product has the ability to continue to provide benefits for me during the pay-off period. For example: computers, desks, copiers, and software programs all continue to provide benefit long after you have paid for them. (Obviously, if you pay off your credit cards at the end of the month, buying consumables on these cards is perfectly acceptable. This advice is for the individual who doesn't make a habit of paying off their cards every month.)

Warning Sign #4

You are using the revenue from seminar sales that haven't happened yet to pay for your current operating costs. This is possibly one of the most dangerous things to do in a speaking business. If you are selling tickets to events in the future, and channeling that revenue to pay for current business needs, be aware by the time the seminar comes around, that money won't be available for the seminar expenses or the inevitable refunds requested by people who have changed their minds. If you want your speaking business to be successful and strong, the most effective financial model is this: All monies for seminar sales should be placed in an escrow account and only released to your business after the successful completion of the event.

The obvious argument against this is that you need these funds to operate your business and stay afloat. If this is the case, a happy medium would be to have a clearly stated non-refundable deposit in your registration form. (If you haven't yet downloaded my seminar registration form that has this clause clearly in print, you can get it here: www.tophersbook.com/regform

This non-refundable deposit needs to accommodate any sales commissions as well as enough to cover your operating expenses. But the majority of the monies need to go in escrow. This will be hard to do initially. The first few events may seem nearly impossible to do without these funds. But I can assure you, if you have the discipline to push past this temporary pain, you will be forever grateful for this advice, and become a seminar company that is a force to be reckoned with.

If you can prevent these four warning signs from happening, or at the very least, notice them immediately when they start and correct them immediately, you will be exercising a strong business acumen that will give you the best possible chance for success in the speaking world.

CHAPTER 23

WHAT A TOOL!

Depending upon what type of speaker you are branding yourself as, you may or may not want to use visual aids like PowerPoint slides for PC or keynote slides for Mac. In the chapter, "How Powerful Are Your Points?" we covered how to use slides to make the right impact and compliment you as a speaker rather than overshadow your words. Now I'm going to address the second key element: the type of projector you are going to use. This may even be more important than the slides because, remember, if you have the wrong type of projector, the audience may not even be able to see the slides.

Depending upon how you market yourself as a speaker, you may or may not be in charge of supplying the projector. But even if you aren't responsible for supplying the projector, you are responsible for making sure the type of projector they supply for you is acceptable to your needs.

Case Study

I was presenting my "Winning the Game of Wealth" seminar in London through a promoter. They were in charge of the A/V. Sound equipment, projectors, lighting, you name it, they took care of it. This was my first major event with this promoter and I had seen their production quality in the past so did not address any of the normal criteria I would for a new promoter with regard to the quality of the A/V equipment. Big mistake.

The morning of the event I showed up and they were using projectors way too weak for the size of audience we had (nearly 300 in attendance) and one of the projectors was so old the color red was no longer projecting. Of course, I used red in some of my text. That text was now invisible on the slides due to the poor projector. The irony, of course, was that the seminar was teaching the concepts of Wealth Creation, and because of the promoter's lack of understanding or attention to detail regarding projectors, the seminar ended up visually looking quite cheap.

This case study provides two valuable lessons for you to take away today.

#1. Make sure you ALWAYS have the projector specifications outlined in contracts with your promoters. For example, in my contract I specifically describe the size and quality of projector necessary for the size of audience estimated, and they are required by signature to supply said projectors.

If you do not yet have a copy of this contract, remember, you can get a copy of it for free simply by filling out my brief survey: www.tophersbook.com/contract

#2. Make sure you ALWAYS use the contract you have created for booking your events. In this case, the promoter was a friend and while we both agreed we should have a contract, neither of us initiated the paperwork. Had I done this, the embarrassing projectors would have never been used.

You... Light Up My Life...

(This sub-title is most effective if you hum the tune while you read it.)

So, what type of projectors should you use? For the most part, the various brands all offer similar features, although I've always been quite happy with BenQ projectors. They seem to project great quality but are typically more affordable than the name brands like Sanyo or Sony. Regardless of the brand name you use, remember this... LUMENS ARE EVERYTHING!

The term, "lumens" refers to how bright the projector is. I've seen this hundreds of times. The projector a speaker is using is too dim for the room, so they go to the adjustments and play around with the brightness and the contrast. The term "brightness" as used in a projector setting does not actually make the projector brighter. It simply adds more white light to the colors, which then need to be compensated by increasing the contrast, leading to usually a poor visual representation of what you see on the notebook screen making the text or images virtually unrecognizable during the presentation.

Here Are Some Standards When Selecting a Projector

Use a projector with a minimum 3,000 lumens for audiences up to 100 people; use a projector with a minimum 5,000 lumens for audiences over 100 people. These are just guidelines and depending on the room, even a 3,000 lumens projector may not be enough if there is fluorescent lighting in the room.

Fluorescent lighting is a projector's worst enemy. If there are fluorescent lights in the room you are speaking in, you will need to have maintenance disconnect them or turn the ones directly above the screen off. Now I've yet to see a venue designed with a speaker in mind, so the fluorescent lights above a screen will most likely be wired to all the other lights. If you turn the fluorescents above the screen off, they all shut off in the room. But this could create another problem with people falling asleep. Typically, the only acceptable solution is to unscrew the fluorescent lights by having maintenance get out a ladder and disconnect them. They will usually tell you it can't be done. This response is born from laziness and is not true. Demand it from them and they will eventually buckle and get maintenance out to unplug the lights. Over half the time, I just pull up a table, stand a chair on it, and unplug them myself. It's usually faster and I get less hassle from the hotel.

The standard projector that I use for all my mid-sized events (less than 100 people) is a 4,000 lumens projector and it just barely gets by in the worst-case scenarios. The next projector I purchase will be a minimum of 5,000 lumens. By the way, the size of 5,000 lumens projectors is getting smaller and smaller so it makes them much easier for transportation where even five years ago, a 5,000 lumens projector was the size of a small car (just a slight exaggeration).

New or Used?

The start-up speaker is usually trying to save money wherever they go. Saving money and buying used projectors is a BAD idea. Traditionally, the bulb for a projector will run between $300 on the low end and $1,200 on the high end. By the time you buy the used projector—which always has an overused bulb ready to explode—and purchase the new bulb, you will have spent nearly the same amount as a new projector anyway. Just buy new.

How Much Is Too Much?

Interestingly, the price of projectors never seem to go down, but every year you end up getting more and more for the same price. For example, 10 years ago the state-of-the-art projectors had about 1,800 lumens and cost around $5,000. Today the top projectors are still around $5,000 but now they are 5,000 lumens and can be run wirelessly from your computer. A good forecast in your business would be to expect to pay about $5,000 every couple years for a new projector and, depending upon how many hours you use your projector, you'll purchase one or two new bulbs during that time as well.

To Rent or Buy?

Does $5,000 sound like a lot of money? If you rent a projector, they typically cost around $400 to $750 per day and if you conduct more than 10 speaking days per year, it will be cheaper in the long run to just purchase a projector. Trust me. Don't rent; buy. It's much more affordable and besides, you'll have a great projector for a home theatre at your house when you aren't speaking.

Where Should I Shop?

Whatever you do, DO NOT PAY RETAIL! I can save you typically 20% by just directing you to some great online shops. I always purchase my projectors from the ProjectorPeople.com website. I've never had one problem with their projectors, they ship very quickly, and being the notoriously cheap shopper that I am, they have consistently proven to provide the best projectors for the cheapest prices.

CHAPTER 24

PROTECTING YOUR INTELLECTUAL PROPERTY

There is a term in business called SWOT: Strength, Weakness, Opportunity, and Threat. Any successful business needs to identify all of these elements in order to stay ahead of the game. Today we are going to tackle the T in SWOT, the biggest threat to professional speakers is the theft of their intellectual property. This theft occurs in two main places:

1. **www.arrrrgggh-matey!.com**

Those Pirating websites like www.torrents.com, www.napster.com, and www.thepiratebay.com just to name a few, have every audiobook, DVD, and inspirational CD ever made by any professional speaker who has made a significant impact in the business. Statistically, the majority of the people reading this eBook right now have downloaded something off of these websites, and the majority of the people who do so are in denial that this is theft. Make no mistake, when you download products from these sites, you are stealing from the person who created the product.

As an example of this, I used to sell a musical CD specifically designed for visualization. I sold more than 5,000 copies worldwide which doesn't sound too bad until you realize that more than 40,000 people stole it off of Torrents. That equated to $998,000 in missed revenue for my company. Could I press legal charges against Torrents? Yes, but I and several other speakers in the business have contacted Torrents to have our products removed and their response was, in so many words. "We aren't taking them off, and go ahead and sue us. Bigger companies have tried, and they've all failed, you will, too."

Unfortunately, I don't have a great solution for this dilemma currently. The only thing I can share with you is how you can adapt to this unfortunate reality. The days of making products that provide long-term and reliable residual income are over. In today's market, you have about a two-month window of opportunity to sell your products to the market before these virtual pirates will steal it. (I had several other adjectives for these people, but my staff made me stick with the politically correct term.) Oh and if you've ever downloaded products yourself from these sites, you are also a pirate, it's not just the people who own the websites.

I'm only aware of two ways to protect you and slow the process of theft as much as possible. Currently, there is no way to eliminate it. If someone is committed to stealing your product, they will find a way.

For Your Inconvenience

Make it as inconvenient as possible to download the product. Having all of your products only available in streaming format can do this. YouTube is a great example of this. Yes, it's possible to download videos from YouTube, but 95%+ of the population has no clue how to do it.

If all of your products are streamed using a similar technology, it will greatly reduce the speed of theft. This comes at a price though. You cannot charge as much for streaming product as you can for physical product.

Price Your Products Affordably

Price your products so affordably people are willing to pay the price tag in order to maintain their ethics. iTunes is a great example of this. They gambled that if you made downloading music super simple, high quality, –with a great user experience, all the while making it affordable, the songs were only 99 cents originally, people would be willing to buy the song instead of search for a stolen version online.

2. **Keep Your Friends Close; Keep Your Colleagues Even Closer**

The second biggest source of theft to professional speakers is amateur and unethical speakers. And this is the one I most want to communicate to you. If you are reading this book, there is a very good chance that you are still breaking into the business and you need to realize that if your presentations are merely re-presentations of the information you gleaned from your favorite speakers, you are also guilty of theft.

Case Study #1

When I was still new to the business, I went to a seminar taught by a British speaker named David Shephard. In his presentation, he had a wonderful story about how he would take apart radios as a child because he wanted to see where the music came from. It was a wonderful metaphor that paralleled tapping into the unconscious mind and I loved it. So much so that I decided to tell the same story to my audiences. Thankfully, I didn't share the story more than three times before I had a career-changing, embarrassing lesson. I got a phone call from an audience member about a month after my presentation. He went to another seminar, this time taught by, you guessed it, David Shephard.

He heard the exact same story (although told much better by Dave) and went up to Dave during the break and asked him if I trained him because he had heard the same story from me a month earlier! Dave politely replied, "No he's actually a student of mine." I was more than humiliated—I was ashamed of myself. It was perhaps one of the most humbling events in my career and I cherish that experience because I learned very early on the dangers of stealing other speaker's material.

And to show you how out of control this theft of intellectual property is in the business, this story has a part II as well. In 2006 I was co-teaching a speakers training seminar in London with another professional speaker who was quite well known and had a thriving business. I shared with the audience the exact same story I just shared with you. The other speaker was on the stage with me as he heard me begin my story. When I mentioned Dave's name (who had also trained this other speaker) and his story about tearing apart radios, the other trainer on stage interrupted with a comment, "Yeah, I have a similar story from my childhood as well that I tell my audience." His face turned beet red as he made the comment, trying to cover his tracks but it was painfully obvious to me, as well as anyone in the audience with the slightest bit of sensory acuity, that the "similar story" he had as a child was a blatant theft of Dave's story as well. Unfortunately, for this other speaker, I'm not sure he ever learned the lesson as I've heard he still tells the story and acts like it actually happened to him as a child.

Case Study #2

Recently, I was asked to speak with an organization in Orange County, CA. At the end of the presentation a young man approached me and asked me if he could interview me for his coaching program. Later that week I looked over his website and was shocked to see that the text of his website was surprisingly similar to that of a good friend of mine in the UK, who is an expert Marketing Coach for Business Consultants, Daniel

Bradbury. Now when I say shockingly similar, it was so bad I called my friend Dan. I asked him if he knew who the kid was or if he had contracted him to represent his technology in the United States. After a bit of digging, he discovered that the young man was a customer of his who had bought a few programs and subscribed to some of his mailings. Daniel went to his website and confirmed my suspicions, but it was worse than I had thought. His ad copy wasn't similar to Daniels website, IT WAS THE EXACT SAME TEXT! His biography and services were identical, his special bonuses were the ones he received from Daniel, and then he just turned around and made them his bonuses for his own clients. It was the most blatant display of plagiarism I have seen in this business, which leads me to the next strategy to prevent your intellectual property from being stolen (assuming that you actually have intellectual property, if you resonate more with the young kid in this story than you do with Daniel, then you are still just the thief—go back to the creative drawing board):

Enforce your intellectual property with voracity! When Daniel discovered this violation, he immediately sent a firm email to the young man clearly stating that his website needed to be changed immediately or he would face legal consequences. The website was changed within the week.

I'm all for being abundant. I'm all for knowing that the universe is unlimited and there is more than enough to go around for everyone, and in business, like you would in your home, you still need to protect what is rightfully yours. If someone came into your home and stole your television because they didn't have one of their own yet you would not say, "it's okay, I'll just come from a space of abundance and go buy a new TV." You would go to the person who stole your TV and demand it back. The same strategy should be applied in your business. I've learned this the hard way.

I had a former student of mine take more than just a story—he took my identity. He started speaking in Australia and his entire presentation was telling people about the trials and tribulations of his life. The only challenge is they weren't his trials and tribulations; they were mine! I didn't pursue him when I found out about it because my thinking was that he was in Australia and it was so far away from my market it wouldn't matter. Now I'm booked to speak all over Australia, and when I share with people my life's story I constantly have people coming up at the breaks asking me if I was trained by my former student. I politely say, "No, he's actually a student of mine." And that's all I have to say and they can do the math.

This chapter has many lessons to be gained. Learn to protect your intellectual property but just as importantly make sure you don't take someone else's. It will ALWAYS catch up with you in the long run.

CHAPTER 25

SELLING YOUR SEMINARS

There is one key element in selling seminars that you MUST adhere to. If you do, you will prosper; if you do not, you will struggle financially for the entirety of your training career. The absence of this one key element is the reason why 90% plus of all seminar companies go broke. Whatever you do, however you market, remember this one powerful rule:

NEVER SELL LIKE YOU LIKE TO BE SOLD!

Instead…

Sell Like Humans Need to be Sold

When I got into the business, I was terribly naïve. I read my first personal development book when I was 12 years old and by the time I entered the field of professional speaking, I had already in my short life read more self-help books than people twice my age. I was passionate about becoming the best I could be, so any opportunity presented to me that would help me better myself was an easy sale. I was what we refer to in the business as a "lay down." I foolishly believed that everyone thought as I did, and to present to a group of people the opportunity to better themselves would be met with equal optimism and eagerness. Turned out, I was way wrong. I'm not alone either.

This is one of the biggest mistakes I see in would-be speakers. They believe that selling seminars will be easy and the money will flow in quickly. After all, who wouldn't want to better themselves? That would have to be the easiest sale in the world right? Well, no actually. In fact, it's probably one of the most difficult. Yes, you are selling the opportunity for someone to better their life, but you are also putting at risk their current way of life. And to the subconscious mind, that can be a very frightening thing.

As much as I would like to think I learned this lesson early on in my career, the fact is, I ignored the obvious signs and continued to think that the reason why people weren't signing up in droves was simply because I hadn't placed myself in front of the right crowds. The fact is, my stubbornness and refusal to see it the way it is lasted way beyond just the beginning of my career... honestly; it stayed with me throughout over half of my career. (I'm what they call a "slow learner.")

There are forces at work stronger than you. Obey them. Everyone who will attend your course will do so for his or her own unique reasons. No matter what those reasons are, they will not buy anything unless they have the following four criteria present in their state of mind:

1. Pain in the Present
2. Hope in the Future (connected to...)
3. Faith in Your Promise
4. A Sense of Urgency

No matter what their buying strategy might be, these four forces will be at work tugging at the human psyche. You need to recognize this and honor it. It will be your natural inclination to think that people will sign up for your programs as quickly and as easily as you bought this book. You are the exception! Most 'normal' people need to be sold, not told. The paradox, of course, is that while most people need to be sold, those very same people hate to be sold.

Pain in the Present

Just imagine for a moment you have had your favorite meal delivered to your door from your favorite restaurant. Your friend who is with you just had their favorite meal delivered from their favorite restaurant. Your meal is cooked to perfection. Every bite dances on your tongue and sends shivers of happiness down your spine. You can't help but to smile as you experience all the different flavors and textures. Your friend, who is with you is eating a different meal from a different restaurant, and says, "Wow, this is really good, do you want to try some?" Now, you are so caught up in the excellent meal before you, and it's making you feel so good, why would you want to try another dish that you have never eaten? I'm sure it's good, but it's not as good as yours. Right?

The fact is you just don't know, but if you are completely satisfied with what you are already eating, your desire to try something new will be significantly diminished. The challenge is that your friend has eaten at your favorite restaurant before, and they've had your favorite dish as well. The reason they ordered their current selection from a different restaurant is because they already know it's far better than the meal you are currently eating. They know your experience would be so much better if you would have just ordered the same meal they did, but you couldn't be more disinterested.

Now imagine that, as you continue to relish in the deliciousness of your meal, you notice an interesting texture in your mouth. It's not normal, it feels out of place, you roll it toward the front of your mouth with your tongue and grasp it with your thumb and forefinger. As you pull it out, you see a long black hair about 10 inches long. Clumps of your favorite food are hanging from the hair and in an instant your stomach moves in unfavorable ways. Your friend turns to you and says, "Yeah, that's why I stopped eating at that restaurant a long time ago. Too many hairs in the food."

A few weeks go by and your friend is over at your house once again. You decide to have delivery to your door, your friend says, "Hey, why don't you try my restaurant, the food is way better, and I'm telling you, you're gonna love it!" Now how much more open are you to trying their restaurant? I would guess that your motivation is much higher now, and that's exactly how a seminar is for most people. It's that new untried restaurant that only the people who have already eaten from there realize just how much better it is. But if your clients' life is already perfect as it is, they won't be very motivated to switch lives. Before you go selling your seminar to someone, you might want to make sure they know about the stray hairs in their life.

NOTE: DO NOT THROW A BUNCH OF STRAY HAIRS IN THEIR LIFE WHEN THEY AREN'T LOOKING!!!

Your job isn't to make their life bad, **your job is to simply point out the places in their life that based on their own admission, aren't working very well. Once you do that, they will be far keener on the idea of trying out a new life.**

Hope in the Future

Here's where it becomes a delicate balance that can take some time to master. If you spend too much time talking about how bad their life currently is, you may sabotage your success by making them feel hopeless, and a hopeless prospect will not buy. They must feel that even though their life currently isn't as great as it could be, they still need to know that it can be great or even greater.

Here's where it gets really tricky. If you help your client to have a sense of hope toward their future, but you forget the third criteria, they still won't buy. You see if you leave them with a sense of hope that they can turn their life around, they won't buy your seminar either, because they haven't linked up their hopeful future to the most important element of all—YOUR SEMINAR!

Faith in Your Promise

Once they are aware that they have some stray hairs in their life, and they feel hopeful that they can get rid of them, you must attach that hope to your seminar promise, and then they must have faith that you can deliver on said promise.

The best way to get someone to attach faith to your promise is by hearing from people that were just like them, who were thinking the exact same things. So make sure you have testimonials, or even better yet, people who have attended your previous seminars and can vouch for your good name. The more testimonials you can provide, the better your sales will be.

A great example of this would be the Anthony Robbins Personal Power series sold all over the world through his infomercials. If you step back and look at all of his 30-minute infomercials, you will discover that 95% of the program is testimonials from people of all different walks of life. This is to ensure that at least one testimonial will speak to someone increasing their chances of success.

A Sense of Urgency

Lastly, if the prospect does not feel that these stray hairs need to be removed from their life immediately, the chance of them signing up will be very limited. You would never continue to eat your meal and just think, "I'll chew around the stray hairs" would you? No way. So how can you create the same level of urgency in their life to create the change? One of the simplest ways is to have them recognize how long they've had the stray hairs, and, more importantly, how many times they've vowed to get it fixed, and, even most importantly, how much less time they have now to fix the problem than when they realized that they had it 5, 10, or 15 years ago.

Overcoming Resistance

If you struggle with selling, I can recommend some excellent books. I didn't write these, I read them, just like you should as well. I can put my hand to my heart and tell you with absolute certainty that these books are my favorite books on influence of all time. I've included the amazon. com links for your purchasing convenience:

These are amazing books, and I love them all: www.tophersbook. com/booklist

If your prospects feel the four emotional criteria mentioned above, there is a good chance they will sign up for your programs. If they are missing just one of them, then the likelihood of registration will be slim to none and I can almost guarantee that you will hear the worst word in the business from your prospect. What is that word?

There is a word in the training business that absolutely must take every step necessary to avoid hearing if you want to become a professional speaker.

Contrary to this evil word, if you do create an environment where your prospect experiences the four criteria, you will hear a completely different word. It's one of the best words a speaker could ever hear when someone is considering attending an event. This one magical, wonderful, exciting word will open the doors of true wealth a speaker.

What are these two words? The first word, the one that is destructive, evil, and paved on the path to poverty is the word...

"Maybe"

This word is absolutely the worst thing you could possibly hear when trying to sell someone a seminar. Here's why: It gives you a false sense of hope that a sale is coming. The problem with a maybe is that you can't do anything with it. It's not an agreement to buy, it's not an objection not to buy that you can overcome. It's this sales purgatory that keeps your time, hopes, and resources all tied up in something that rarely if ever goes anywhere.

But 'maybe' does have some positive sides to it as well. It keeps you hopeful, kind of like when an actor gets nominated for an Academy Award or when a good-looking person gives you their phone number. There's a lot of optimism and anticipation in what might happen, but no matter how great it makes you feel, the nomination for an award and the phone number in your hand do absolutely nothing for you if you don't win or don't make the call. So if you want to feel good but go nowhere, be happy with a "maybe." If you want to make some money in this business, you need to hear the most enjoyable word ever with regard to selling a training program.

This one magical word can be music to your ears. When you hear it, it virtually guarantees your bank account is going to grow. What is that word? It's the best word anyone in sales could ever hear. And the word is...

"No"

That's right, it's a "no." Why on earth would the word "no" be so enjoyable? Because it's tangible. You can work with a "no." Unlike a maybe which doesn't have any outcome at all, if someone is professional enough to tell you "no," you can then find out why. In the world of selling anything, remember this one phrase:

"No doesn't really mean NO!"

Typically, "no" just means, "I have questions." And since we haven't had the opportunity to answer those questions, the prospect does not want to take any action. But this is where you can really help them.

Instead of thinking about how you can overcome their objections, approach it from the perspective that you want to understand their world view, and you want to answer any questions that they may have. By doing this, you are serving your future customer in the best way possible.

Once you answer their questions, the "no" will often become a "yes." But be careful, you also don't want to spin your wheels answering a bunch of questions that are irrelevant to the cause. In other words, only overcome the objection, or answer the questions that actually lead to the sale. In many cases, a person will ask a series of irrelevant questions to keep from having to make a commitment once they are answered. So here are some quick catch phrases that will assist you in getting to the real questions that prevent someone from committing to your program.

As soon as someone says they don't want to go to your program...

"Okay then. Thank you so much for your honesty, I can't tell you how many times someone doesn't give me the courtesy of a polite 'no.' It's refreshing. So that I may continue to improve my program and offer the best possible service, would you mind if I ask you what made you decide you don't want to attend? I imagine other people might share in your opinion, and I'd like to make sure I satisfy those needs in my program. For what reason did you decide this wasn't for you?"

The answer to this question will reveal one of three things: #1. what your program is lacking, #2. what your program has that is a turn-off, or #3. what part of your program you forgot to mention so the client is unaware that your program actually does cover the information that they find of value. Either way, this is very valuable information, and, regardless of whether or not they change their mind, this information will prove to be very valuable for you in the future when you are speaking with people.

#1 Your Program is Lacking Something

"That's very good information. Thank you very much. My course does not cover that, so I'd say you made a very wise decision. May I ask you another question? If in the future we decide to add that information into our course, then would you want to attend?"

#2 Your Program has a Turn-Off

"Wow, thank you for your honesty. I can appreciate that you don't like _____. I know I've been to a lot of seminars in my day where I couldn't stand parts of the program, so I can completely relate to your resistance, and you know, during those programs, I usually had one of two outcomes. The first outcome was that I resisted the information and consequently didn't get any value from it, the other outcome was when I realized it's okay to not enjoy certain portions of programs, but it's important to still stay open-minded to the lessons available during that portion. You see, the interesting thing about that part of the program is that for one, it's only a part of the program, and that part is designed to help you [insert one of their goals]. And so I know you won't enjoy that part of the program as much as the other parts. I get that. I guess my question for you though is this. Wouldn't it be worth experiencing that one part of the program even if you don't like it, if it can ultimately lead

you toward [repeat their goal mentioned above]? Seems to me that would be worth it. Don't you?"

#3 They Want Something They Think Your Program is Lacking, But it Actually Has It

"Really? That's important to you? Let me ask you a question, just suppose my program actually did cover that. If you knew you would get it by attending my program, then would you want to come? That's great, because my program actually covers that. Now I'm not trying to pull a fast one here and just throw anything into my program that I think you may want. I sincerely do cover that in the program, I simply forgot to mention it. We cover that during the [insert what segment] segment and I promise you'll be thrilled at the information on that topic."

Okay, those are some phrases that can get you started. Mastering the art of sales will have several dips in it. Remember, it's worth pushing through the dip. If you don't, you'll just be average, and nobody wants to be average in selling. That's a road to poverty. Instead, be the best in your world at what you do, and commit to pushing through the sales dip so you can affect the lives of many more people on this small planet.

CHAPTER 26

HOW TO SPIN A CANCELLATION

t's two weeks before your big event. Your campaign was a successful one and you've got the perfect number of people enrolled to your event. You are so excited. You know that with this many in attendance, you will enjoy some profit for this event and that your sales for future events should be substantial. You couldn't be happier

As you check your morning messages, you discover there are two people calling you to explain that they have a personal emergency they have to attend to, and they cannot attend but are deeply sorry and really wish they could make it. You're saddened to hear of their plight, but reschedule them for a future event or refund them their tuition based on your refund policies.

By the end of the week, three more have cancelled! During the week before the event another seven people call in and, all of a sudden, your perfect event now has 12 less people scheduled to attend. Your catering order is now overbooked. The venue you hired is too large for the small audience you will now be expecting. Your refunds have depleted your bank account and you are in panic mode.

I hope this situation never happens to you, but if there's one thing I'm certain about in the speaking business it's this: If you have an event scheduled, I can promise you that people will be canceling.

I've mentioned before how I'm always amazed at how many people have personal emergencies two weeks before an event. The amount of grandmothers and grandfathers who meet their timely demise right before an event is suspiciously high. You might even say, it's unbelievably high. Why does this occur two weeks outside of every event?

Simply put, because when people are going to attend a seminar, subconsciously they realize that the program is going to task them to do things which will change their lives, and for most people, that change is scary and brings about uncertainty. Now depending upon the type of seminar you offer, this phenomenon of high cancellations may not be as severe. Generally speaking, the more your seminar focuses on personal development, the higher the cancellations you will experience.

Depending upon what type of cancellation policy you have, your financial stability may be in jeopardy—which is why you might be interested in my registration enrollment form, complete with iron-clad refund policy. If you haven't yet done so, visit www.tophersbook.com/regform to order it. You will save yourself thousands of dollars in the long run. But there is a deeper problem than even your financials. If you allow these people a way out, you aren't fulfilling your purpose in life.

When you let someone off the hook, you are enabling their fears and reinforcing their current situation in life. Would you be willing to risk looking like the 'bad guy' in order to fulfill your mission of empowering people and helping them to improve their lives? This will be one of the key testing points in your career as to whether you are in the business for the right reasons or simply hear to enjoy the praise and applause. Sometimes, in order for people to get the change that they want and need, you may temporarily need to be the one they resent.

This is a business, and if someone makes a commitment to you, they should honor that. But beyond that you will need to re-enroll people into their reasons for attending your events because that's the only way they will get the change they desire.

So here are some tips on how you can re-enroll people into a seminar that they already committed to attend:

I realize there are RARE cases where the person who is trying to back out is doing so for legitimate reasons and no matter what you say or do, they just simply will not be able to attend. This advice is not for these people, it's for the ones who are lying to you about their reasons, and deep down, just don't want to go anymore due to laziness, lack of motivation, fear, or distraction. The challenge here is, how do you know which ones are which? Well, you probably never will. But suffice it to say that if their reasons are legitimate, these techniques I'm about to share with you won't work. If these techniques do work, then they were probably not being forthright in their reasons for not attending.

I'm going to address how to get the maximum number of registrants to your events from two different perspectives—one from the aspect of preventative maintenance and two from the aspect of damage control.

Preventative Maintenance

You need to prepare your clients in advance to expect that their fears, friends, work, and lovers will challenge them and try to keep them from attending. Whenever someone signs up for my seminar, I have a discussion either live or via email about what to expect now that they have enrolled, and cancellations are radically diminished. When I omit this process, the cancellations are always much higher.

I tell them about how their fears will be disguised as circumstances that they will think are beyond their control. I let them know that this is just natural human behavior and they aren't broken or wrong, but if they don't find a way to overcome that circumstance, they will remain stuck in their present situations. In other words, you need to have them get excited about these challenges that everyone experiences before attending the course. Give them specific instructions as well. Tell them things like, *"when this happens I want you to call me immediately so you and I can come up with a solution that lets you still attend the program."* When all this takes place up front, the amount of cancellations will significantly drop.

One of the ways that I have made sure this conversation always takes place is I have a downloadable .mp3 file that is an audio pep talk for them to listen to. It gets them excited for the event and it diminishes the likelihood of cancellations. Since I've implemented this audio download, I've noticed that my cancellations drop by approximately 60% . That is staggering when you consider the average cost of events.

What's even better about the audio download is that I made it generic for the event and date and topic so I can use the same audio download for all my programs. But not just my programs, but for anyone's programs. I used to sell audio download for $24.95 but through this book, I'm offering this audio download that you may use with your business for free: www.tophersbook.com/nocancel

Damage Control

Okay, so you didn't get the audio download, and you forgot to have a conversation, or if you did, it wasn't effective. Now all of a sudden you start getting people calling up and trying to cancel. What do you do?

The first thing that MUST occur is you need to interrupt their pattern. Right now they are simply running a pattern of fear, laziness, distraction, intimidation, or something else; what the pattern is called is irrelevant. The fact is you must break it. And whatever the pattern is, it will typically be laced with a fear that you are going to challenge them on the cancellation, that's why they made the story for why they cannot attend as juicy and as detailed as possible. So how do you interrupt the pattern? I do it by one statement followed up with asking them a question. It doesn't matter what their excuse is for canceling either. The statement and question is always the same. *"Okay, no problem, if you can't attend, you can't attend, so we'll make sure we cross your name off the list. So now that that's out of the way, I'd like to ask you a question, and I think it's going to give you a lot of comfort in this situation as well. Would you mind if I ask you a question? What was it that made you enroll to this seminar in the first place?"*

The purpose of this question is to re-engage them into why they signed up, and by doing so, they will access the same emotional state that got them to a yes in the first place. By the way, in that statement above I never said I would give them their money back, I simply said we would cross their name off the list. This will be sufficient to put them at ease.

Once they are re-engaged to their reasons, you need to bring those reasons to the present situation. So I ask them, *"… and has that situation changed in your life or is that still important to you?"* The answer will be yes if they are being honest with you. *"So then your reasons for attending this course are still as real today as they were when you signed up, you just have something getting in the way now."* They will agree. *"May I share with you some insights that you may or may not be aware of right now?"* They will say yes. *"Great. You know, I've been running seminars for _____ years now, and there's one pattern that ALWAYS surfaces in this business. There are no exceptions, and it's as predictable as the seasons. The pattern that I see all the time is that the one thing that people need to get the most from a training is the one thing that will prevent them from attending. For example, you want to go to this seminar to help you [restate their reasons for attending] and now the very reason you don't think you can attend is because* [restate their reasons for canceling] *but can you see how those two are directly related?* [This is where you have to think on your feet a bit and connect the two, but trust me. There's always a connection.]

At this point you will be off script and just need to connect with them and be a great listener. But the main point is to let them know that overcoming these reasons is the very act they need to send to the universe to have that issue stop creeping up in their lives. This is the best gift you could ever give them and will serve them far better than letting them off the hook.

CHAPTER 27

THE SLOT MACHINE OF THE SPEAKING WORLD

Over the past 30 years, I've met a lot of speakers. From newbie start-up speakers filled with optimism and certainty that they will become the next Anthony Robbins all the way up to, well... Anthony Robbins. In that 30-year span, I've never once heard a speaker claim that they are perfect. I've never once heard a speaker tell the audience that all of the speakers on the circuit come from a space of abundance and live the principles that they themselves teach 24/7. So I can't say that the biggest lie ever created by speakers is that we are perfect, but I can say the biggest lie speakers have never tried to dispel is that we are perfect.

The majority of speakers on the circuit today are there because they saw a speaker in their past that inspired them to want to do the same. By far, this profession is one of the most rewarding ever invented. We don't sell snake oil, we sell the dream of reaching your dreams. And that can be pretty intoxicating to anyone. But make no mistake. ALL speakers have their shortcomings. We all forget to live the very principles we teach from time to time. For some of us, probably more often that we would care to admit.

You can bet that if someone teaches people how to have a great relationship with their partner, they will have struggles in their relationships as well. If someone teaches people how to live a healthy lifestyle, they occasionally eat something unhealthy. If someone teaches principles on wealth creation, they have had and will have financial challenges in the future. Why? Because **professional speakers are just like other people, only louder.**

It's so easy to see a speaker up on stage and think that they are living the perfect life with no emotional issues, no financial challenges, and no secret weakness for a snack that isn't healthy, but nothing could be further from the truth. In this chapter, we are going to address the financial aspect of a speaker's life.

This is a highly competitive business. There is no shortage of speakers who will accept an offer from a promoter for less than you want to charge. Speakers have essentially become commodities and our value is determined by simple supply and demand. That supply and demand will fluctuate based upon the success of your last book, the reviews of your last audio program, or the viral nature of your last video. So when supply is up, and demand is low, how can you maintain your level of financial stability? The same way casinos do.

Casinos are brilliantly run businesses. They know which games produce the highest level of revenue for the house. They also know which ones are their biggest risks. They strategically place the high-risk games among a sea of lower-risk activities that will drive in a more stable level of revenue. What is that revenue for a casino?

The Slot Machine

Slot machines statistically have the lowest level of payout and the highest level of income for a casino—if not the highest, certainly the most stable and predictable. In fact, it's been said, (probably apocryphal), the slot machines produce enough revenue to pay for the expenses of the entire casino each month! Speakers have just such a secret weapon. That secret weapon is none other than our products.

Audio and video programs, books, and subscriptions are the most profitable portion of our business. So much so that many speakers have devoted the majority of their business to marketing their products online and have virtually neglected their live trainings to simply sell product through the Internet.

A speaker who offers a live training with no product to sell is like a casino with no slot machines; they could make a profit, but the risk of that not happening is extremely high and most if not all of their profit will be left to chance. To put it simply, if you aren't selling product at your seminars, you are missing out on a huge revenue stream. And just as badly, you are not serving your customers as well as you could because if you think someone can attend your program and implement all that you share with them without any follow-up learning is naïve and irresponsible at best. If you really want your audience to walk away with the highest possible chance of success, then they need to walk away with a follow-up plan. That follow-up plan is through products—audio, video, books, or subscriptions.

Creating Your Product

When I see speakers who haven't created any products and I ask them why, the biggest excuse I hear is that they don't have the time to set aside and make their product. This is a lie. Everyone has as much time as they need to do anything. The question is, do you value creating a product enough that you will set aside other projects of less importance? The other reason why someone might not have a product, although they would never admit it, is because they don't have anything original to say and if they were to put their knowledge onto a product, it would be in violation of copyright laws from the person they garnered (stole) their knowledge from in the first place.

By the way, there are plenty of Master Resell Rights products available. These are essentially a "product in a box" that you can purchase, put your name on as the author, and voila! You are now an author. You can have it printed, or use as an eBook, they are both legal and viable ways of producing product rather quickly. The great thing about Master Resell Rights products is that you keep 100% of the sales and owe nothing to the individual you purchased the product from.

When looking for these products, it's important to make sure it's a Master Resell Right, not just a Resell Right. When you own the Master Resell Rights, you can use the product however you wish with no restrictions whatsoever.

For example, I used to sell an eBook called, "Sowing the Seeds of Success." I no longer offer it, since I prefer to discontinue old products as my line evolves. But at its peak, it made me thousands of dollars. I would use it as an up-sell product when people purchased something from my website. On average, 1 out of 5 people buying something online would purchase the suggested up-sell of the book. It was only $5, but that added a nice level of revenue to my bottom line every year.

If you are too busy to write a book or get in to the studio to record, then realize that one of the best places for you to write and record is when you are speaking in front of an audience. You can take a video recording of your seminar, have it transcribed, and you have the makings of your first book. You can take the recording of your seminar, turn it into a downloadable or streaming .mp3, and you have your first audio program. This takes no extra time and very little expense. In fact, if you follow the advice I'm about to share, it won't cost you anything.

Now you might be thinking that people wouldn't want to pay for a recording of an event they are already attending, but if you look into it a bit deeper, you will discover that is EXACTLY what they want.

Look at the number of people who record your seminars on their mobile phones or light scribe digital pens or .mp3 recorders nowadays. The numbers are staggering. Look at how many people hold up their mobile phones and take pictures of your slides for later reference. The reason they do this is because they are yearning for follow-up material. If someone is recording any of your presentation, that shows that they value follow-up materials. You owe it to your audience to provide them those materials. How do you do it?

You create a low-cost, easier alternative than having them record it themselves. Simply record the event and offer the recordings for a small fee. And it doesn't have to be a lot in order to create enough cash flow to produce your first product. If you have 30 people in a room and each of them pays you just $20 for the full day's recording with all of the slides from your presentation included, then you've produced $500 in revenue to pay someone $100 to edit your recordings. It's always a great idea to include something extra that they won't get in the live training to encourage them to purchase your offer.

Interestingly, the biggest reason I hear from speakers as to why they won't record their presentation on video is because they say they aren't as polished as they would like to be and they want to wait and deliver the program four of five times before they get the recording. I'm always shocked at this excuse. Think about it. If you aren't polished enough to record your presentation on video, how can you in good conscience say you are prepared enough to deliver your presentation to a live audience? Are they just your practice group? For me, if I'm not prepared enough to record a video of my presentation, then I'm not prepared enough to deliver the presentation in the first place.

Once you have your first product recorded, how do you want to reproduce it? The answer here is as many ways as possible. Why? Because different people like different avenues of delivery. Some people want to read about ideas, others want to watch videos, and some prefer to listen to them on their mobile devices or in their car. The more ways you have to deliver this information, the better. This is why recording your seminars on video is the best place to start.

Depending upon the length of your seminar, you can pay a transcription service as little as $50 to transcribe your entire event into printed text, giving you a huge jumpstart on your book. If you conduct regular events, each program can be transcribed and you instantly have a subscription service for your customers to receive monthly updates whether they attend your events or not.

If you want to create an audio program, just take the vocal portion from your video and you instantly have your audio program. In fact, even if someone buys your video, you can offer the audio portion only as a bonus so they can listen to it on their mobile audio device or in their car.

Thanks to the advancement of technology, you don't even need to burn the product onto a CD, DVD, or printed material. You can just email them a link to download all of the information, reducing your expenses to produce the product down to labor for editing and/ or transcription. The great thing about this strategy is that you only have to pay for the editing once, but now every time you offer this program in the future, you have a recorded version ready to be delivered immediately to your audience. The revenue you will produce, if done correctly, should pay for your entire seminar expenses, including venue hire, refreshments, transportation, and accommodation.

CHAPTER 28

YOUR DEMO REEL

The Visual One Sheet

As mentioned in the chapter, "One Page, Many Requests," the one sheet for a speaker is one of the most valuable tools for getting booked. Thanks to modern technology, there is another tool that may even surpass the importance of a one sheet. That tool is your demo reel. It's an interesting term—demo reel, since it describes a technology that people don't even use anymore. It should probably just be called a demo video.

Before a company is going to be willing to plop down $10,000 for a speaker, no matter how many raving endorsements you have, they will want to see a sample of you in action. If a company calls you up and asks to see a demonstration, anything short of, "absolutely, I'll FedEx it to you today" or "Of course, you can watch it on my website, here's the link" will most likely cause you to lose the sale.

Now if you do actually have a demo video, and they watch the DVD or click on the link to enjoy it and instead see a poorly produced product, you will also most likely lose the sale.

A few years back, I needed a septoplasty on my nose. This is a surgical procedure to straighten the septum and restore normal breathing to the nasal passage. But because my career is in front of an audience, (actually the real reason is just because I'm vain), I didn't want to just go to a normal Ear, Nose & Throat (ENT) Specialist. I wanted to go to a plastic surgeon. So I had my primary care physician give me several names of well-respected specialists and plastic surgeons. I went to each one and interviewed them. There was one surgeon who was an ENT and a plastic surgeon. He seemed like the perfect choice. He could straighten my nose and shave a little of the top for cosmetic reasons all in one fell swoop. When I went to his office, the place was a bit run down. The chairs were uncomfortable and the big glass industrial-looking doors displayed a view of a parking lot and cars rushing by. The fluorescent lights reminded me of an office space and gave off a very cold vibe. The reception staff was unfit and dressed very casual. I felt like I was sitting in a public aid building, not a plastic surgeon's lobby.

When I met with the surgeon, I was impressed with him as a person, but the environment, from the reception to the procedure room, were all quite stale.

The next office I went to was completely different. As I walked into the lobby, there was rich burl wood accents and plush chairs that made me feel at home. There was a huge tropical fish tank with exotic salt water fish swimming about and the reception staff was professional from head to toe. There was soft classical music being played and vanilla aromatherapy, which made me feel like I was waiting for a spa treatment.

The high-class décor continued into the procedure rooms with warm earth tones and more beautiful people all dressed immaculately. The surgeon spent about one-fifth the time that the other surgeon did and this guy was only a plastic surgeon, he wasn't an ENT specialist. By all rights, the other surgeon was more qualified. As an ENT the previous surgeon could bill half the procedure to my insurance, immediately cutting my personal fees in half. This surgeon in the beautiful spa-like office would end up costing me twice as much because insurance wouldn't cover it, and I hardly got to speak with him! Guess which one I hired? The plastic surgeon in the spa. The environment was as important, if not more important, than the credentials of the surgeon. I somehow felt better in his office—like I was safe, and well taken care of. Would the other surgeon have been as effective? Yes, perhaps even more, but I judged him for the poor environment.

For your customers, your environment will be your demo video. If it is cheaply produced, all of that amateur energy will be associated toward you. So when you get a demo video made, it's worth spending the time to have it professionally recorded and edited.

This doesn't mean you can't have some raw and unedited videos as well. I've got loads of those mobile camera videos on my websites, which help to create a feeling of authenticity, but when someone is considering paying me $10,000 to speak to their company for 45 minutes, I want to make sure they are seeing a video comparable to a $10,000 keynote speaking fee. And you should, too.

Thankfully, because of modern technology you can now get some very acceptable 'professional' videos made personally. The key to a professional looking video is really two things:

1. Quality Sound

The sound should be recorded from a direct feed from your microphone. Do not use an ambient mic that picks up all the noises in the room. Those sounds are okay for picking up laughter and your jokes, and audience applause, but mixed in with that ambient noise you want to have a nice clean audio track of your voice sounding crisp and clean.

2. Quality Lighting

Lighting is critical as well. A demo video should be well lit, and make sure if there is a projection screen that it isn't directly behind you (if it is you will usually just look like a shadow on film). If you have lighting directed at the stage, make sure there are also lights behind you on the ground shining up to eliminate the shadows from the light generated in front of you. I've attempted to light my own stages and I usually fall horribly short of professional. It usually requires someone who is a professional in lighting stages. When it's done right, it just makes your video shine with professionalism.

Beyond a demo video of your presentation, people will want to watch testimonials. Now before you start collecting a bunch of video testimonials with your flip video recorder or your iPhone, you should first ask yourself what your purpose for the video testimonial is going to be.

There are three types of comments you can receive from an audience member:

1. Testimonial—Somebody who talks about how great the speaker is.
2. Quote—Somebody who talks about how great the seminar is.
3. Endorsement—Somebody who talks about how they've applied the techniques they got from the speaker and because of this, they've received specific, tangible results.

While all are important, the Endorsement will typically persuade more people to take action. It's best to discuss these types of comments with the volunteer in advance so they can think about what they would say in each arena. Your interview questions should elicit from them a testimonial, a quote, and an endorsement. This way, you'll be free to edit and select the best of the three.

During the Interview

Make them smile! Have fun with them; demonstrate how much they should smile, if they don't smile enough, start it over, and tell them to do the same thing again, but this time smile. Smiling cannot be emphasized enough!!

Make sure they repeat the question so we know what they are talking about.

Incorrect:

Interviewer: *"What did you think about the value of the course compared to the price you paid?"*

Interviewee: *"It was great! Ten times easily."*

Correct:

Interviewer: *"What did you think about the value of the course compared to the price you paid?"*

Interviewee: *"The value for the course was worth so much more than the cost I paid for it. I would easily have paid 10 times what I did!"*

Don't let them tell jokes or use sarcasm, it doesn't come across well. Sincerity is the only emotion we want them to convey.

Be patient! Don't talk over them. Remember, you will be editing your voice out, so don't cut them off, butt in, or give approving commentary such as, "um hum, yes, excellent, great" or anything of the sort. Give plenty of non-verbal approval while they are talking though, and keep smiling as you listen, it will remind them to keep smiling as they talk to you.

Have a second of silence before and after you ask and they answer the question; this will be greatly appreciated by your editor when you start editing the videos.

Preparing the Volunteer

In order to get them to have fun, smile, and answer the questions appropriately, here's a script to use as a guideline for preparing the person for what to say and how to say it. Say this while smiling really big...

"Okay, so the important thing here is that we want to convey the same enthusiasm and excitement you have received from this program into the testimonial, so do you mind if I give you some tips on how to make a great testimonial, and have a lot of fun in the process? [They'll say yes] *Great, do what I'm doing, smile! It will seem strange perhaps at first, but it looks really good on camera and if you don't do it on camera, you end up looking depressed and too serious, and we want fun and energetic. Can you do that for me?"*

"Now as far as what to say, just say what's in your heart. We want the comments to be sincere, but if you want some guidance, there are typically three types of comments we are looking for. The kind that talk about your opinion of [speaker's name] *and his speaking style, the kind where you comment on what you thought of the seminar and the content covered, and the last would be talking about how you have applied or how you are going to apply a specific portion of the program to produce a specific result in your life. If you've attended the course before, you could use this as an opportunity to talk about how much better your life is in specific areas as a result of some of the information you got from the program. If this is your first time, you could use this as an opportunity to make a public commitment regarding how you are going to apply a specific portion of the program into your life and what type of result you are confident that it will produce. I'll ask you questions about all three if you want to start thinking about how you'll want to answer those."*

"Okay, the next thing is to remember to repeat back my question in a conversational tone, that way we can edit me out so the dialogue sounds more natural. So if I ask you for example, 'Did you receive good money for value at this program?' don't just say 'yes', instead repeat the question back in the conversation. Say something like, 'I got so much value for the price of the course, I would have easily paid 10 times what I paid.' That will make sense to the viewer after I'm edited out, okay?"

"Also, don't focus on the camera, just look at me. Act as if it's just you and I having a normal conversation, and you are trying to convince me to go see this guy named [speaker's name], okay? Alright, let's start, remember to smile big, I know it may not seem or feel natural at first, but it will look way better on tape, so smile big okay?"

Once the camera starts to roll, follow these basic guidelines that will ensure you have some high quality, and usable video endorsements:

On Video Production

- Have them take their name tags off.
- Tell them to spit out their gum.
- Zoom in on their face. Full body and even half-body shots make the person look too small, and typically people talk too much with their hands, which distracts the viewer from the message. So zooming in on their face lets the viewer hear the message

without being distracted by what is going on with their hands or the movement behind them in the scene.

This type of framing makes the subject look small. It's also quite intimidating for someone not used to speaking on camera to look into the lens.

Don't center them in the screen. It looks stale and unemotional. Off-centered, asymmetrical shots convey emotion and interest. Centered frames look like a mug shot.

By zooming in on the client, it creates a more intimate, trustworthy feeling, and now if they move their hands it won't be distracting. By having them look off camera they will feel more at ease and this will show in the recording.

- Don't let them look in the camera lens. Most people get too nervous and screw up their lines. If they are looking off camera at the interviewer, it allows them to stay focused and forget about any camera anxiety they might have.
- Dress 'em up! Don't let them look sloppy. If you need to straighten a collar, do so. If you need to tell them to comb their hair, do so. Also, look for the best-dressed people in the

audience and ask them for a testimonial. If they are dressed sloppy, you probably won't use their testimonial anyway.

- Don't play with the zoom. Once you have them in the frame, try to keep their head the same size. If they back up or move forward, then, of course, modify your zoom to maintain the same size. During editing, it will look jumpy if one second they are zoomed in, and the next they are zoomed out.

- Be aware of what is in the background! If you have a wide open space, it lets people walk in the shot. Try having your company banner, some flowers, or something appealing to the eye in the background, and make sure there aren't any vertical stripes in the background, or behind the person's head you are filming. Vertical stripes can 'confuse' some cameras and it creates an interesting, but undesirable special effect where the lines 'dance' around in the background. If there are vertical lines behind their head (including tree branches), it might create the illusion that they have sticks coming out of their head.

- Make sure to balance the whites on the camera. This is a function called "white balance." This function allows the colors to be more true to life. Without doing this, the picture will sometimes be orange or bluish depending upon what type of lighting you are using. White balance allows the camera to adjust the color based upon what kind of light the room is using. If you are using a camera with this function, simply point the camera at a piece of white paper and push the white balance button. If you don't have a camera that has this function, usually your editor can correct the color later during editing.

- Double-check the sound. Always have a set of "over the ear" headphones available for the cameraperson so they can listen to the sound during the recording (if your camera doesn't allow this, at least play it back immediately after recording while the volunteer is still there to make sure it sounded okay).

You Be the Judge

During the interview, ask yourself this question, "If I were watching what I just saw and heard in this person's comments, would I be compelled to attend?" If the answer is no, give them feedback on what's missing. Now is not the time to be concerned about hurting someone's feelings. Now is the time to coach the individual into the best performance they can do. If they need to do multiple takes, it's okay. When someone agrees or volunteers to provide a video-taped testimonial, they sincerely want it to turn out professional and compelling.

CHAPTER 29

YOU'RE ONLY AS GOOD AS YOUR TEAM

They say it takes a village to raise a child, but when you are organizing your own speaking engagement from beginning to end, it seems like it takes even more than a village; it takes a village, a few acts of God, and some luck of the Irish. But the reality is that it only takes seven people—more accurately, there are seven necessary roles outside of the speaker that need to be covered for a smooth program. Depending on the size of your event, one person can absorb more roles, or the opposite could be true. Several people may need to bear the burden of one role. What are these roles?

Event Manager (EM)

This person is your boss! Make no mistake; at a seminar, you are not in charge, you are simply the monkey on stage making noise. They make the seminar flow and they are the one who people go to for any authority-based requests. As a speaker you need to commit this sentence to memory. *"I'm not in charge, you need to ask _____ for that. They are in the back of the room."* DO NOT under any circumstance make policy changes or exceptions, make promises to individuals, or assume any sort of administrative responsibility. You need to keep your focus on connecting with your audience, and, if need be, inspire them to go to the back of the room to take action with a product or seminar.

This person is in charge of the other six positions. All of the other positions report to the EM, and the EM reports to you. If there is a problem in the seminar, it's the job of the EM to make sure you don't know about it because they have everything under control. They must have strong leadership qualities and be very familiar with your companies policies and procedures. It's best if they are an employee of your company or an independent contractor. After all, they will be making policy decisions for you, make sure you trust them.

Administrative Services Coordinator (ASC)

This position requires someone who is detail-oriented, and has the ability to forecast every possible scenario. I often tell my ASC that their main job is to think of everything that can possibly go wrong during the day and spend their day doing whatever it takes to make sure none of those things they've thought of ever happen.

They are usually the first to arrive and the last to leave, with the possible exception of the Event Manager. Like all of the seven roles, this person has critical things they must do before, during, and after the event, such as making copies for any handouts needed that day, ensure the speaker has ample flipchart paper and working markers, make sure the chairs are organized and ready for any exercise, round up participants after the break, and organize feedback forms, just to name a few.

They have the logistical answers or, at the very least, know who has the answers.

Registration Coordinator (RC)

This position does way more than their job title may indicate. While their primary role is during the registration process before the program begins, they have many other duties during the day to make sure the rosters reflect the correct amount of people in the training. Again, a detail-oriented person is a must, combined with their most important asset: personality. This person MUST be personable, externally focused, and truly care about the well-being of others.

This position also assists any security detail by making sure that everyone sitting in the seminar room has the necessary name tags or wrist bands. Because they are the person/people who are taking registration, make sure they are good with names, because during the event, you'll want them to create a seating chart with all the participants (or as many as they can remember) for the speaker to use during the event.

Personal Assistant to Trainer (PA)

Unlike the previous positions which may have several people involved in the roles and duties, the PA is only one person, unless of course, there is more than one speaker, then you may need more than one PA.

The PA absolutely must have a backbone and the ability to politely and even publicly corral the speaker into doing what they are told and stick to timeframes. For example, Kate Ginn, my event manager in the UK, also takes on the role of my PA, and is literally my shadow during an event. Before the seminar, during breaks, and after the program has ended, she is no more than an arm's reach away to help me if I need anything.

Kate and I have a non-verbal signal that when she sees me make it, it essentially means, "come rescue me!" and she springs into action and escorts me away from the crowd of people wanting to ask me questions. Why would she do this? It usually has something to do with either me having to pee or eat.

She is like a human time machine keeping me on track and on time. She doesn't take any of my guff and despite her barely being 5 feet tall, quite frankly, she scares the crap out of me and I'll do whatever she tells me to do. That's a PERFECT Personal Assistant! While I may have made her sound to be pretty harsh, at the deepest level she truly cares for my well-being and wants to make sure I perform at my best. A great Personal Assistant during a training day will make sure all the bases are covered for the speaker.

Product Sales Representative (PSR)

This is perhaps the most critical position for the entire day when it comes to making a profit. The person or people in charge of product sales MUST have strong personal communication skills, the ability to persuade, and the desire to sell. These are the people behind your sales counter, so you must trust that while you are shaking hands and signing books, they have your bottom line interests top of mind.

They don't just hide behind the counter and take orders. Anyone can do that. They need to mingle during the breaks if people aren't buying. They should be gaining rapport with the participants such to the degree that they can quite comfortably ask them, "So have you thought about coming to the next program?"

The product sales person or team must also have a well-rounded knowledge of your products and services. People buy from people with certainty; they rarely buy from people with ambiguity. If a sales representative is constantly saying things like, "I don't know," "I'm not sure," or "Let me go check, I'll be right back," they will slow down and often kill the sale.

These people MUST have some sales training from you or your Event Manager to get familiar with your product and the sales process. They must be familiar and comfortable with the process of up-selling and down-selling. It's best if they LOVE your products, too. You'll be surprised at how much more product gets sold when the salesperson can honestly rave about their favorite product.

Audio/Video Technician (AV Tech)

If there is a position that you will be out-sourcing to a professional company, this is most likely the one. Your audio/video presentation will often make or break the perception of professionalism that a person has of you and your seminar. It's best to not leave this up to a novice who just likes to listen to music.

Out of all the things that can go wrong in a seminar, audio/video challenges are at the top of the list. Power surges, blown fuses, dead batteries, faulty connections—you name it, it will happen. Projector bulbs love to burn out 30 minutes before the most important presentation of your life. You want to make sure this person knows where a replacement bulb is BEFORE it goes out. They need to have access to local pro-audio shops. If they are comfortable with a soldering iron. all the better!

If you have all of your own A/V equipment, a proper A/V Tech will be able to step in, set up, maintain, and tear down your entire system, no questions asked. As a speaker, the one thing you DO NOT want to be doing before your program is heavy lifting, hauling cable, and running back and forth from the stage to the sound system in the back to adjust the knobs. You'll break a sweat and look like you just ran a marathon when you get on stage. Not a pretty sight!

Security

Don't overdo this one. Keep your ego in check. Nothing looks more silly than having a 300-pound bodyguard standing in front of you, escorting you through a crowd of only 10 people. Obviously, the larger the audience, the more important this becomes, but unless you are a New York Times' bestselling celebrity author, you probably won't be needing a bodyguard. I've spoken to audiences of 5,000 and I've never needed one. My 5-foot PA Kate Ginn is sufficient to escort me to the toilets if need be.

So why do you need security then? To make sure doors are locked, to make sure the cash taken in during the day stays accounted for and gets from where it may be to your briefcase or hotel room. They make sure they know the fire escape routes and are aware of any fire alarm tests that may be happening. They supervise any incidents or injuries and stand in front of your doors in the morning to make sure the doors don't open earlier than advertised.

Get a Checklist

It's taken me nearly 20 years to compile a pre-flight, flight, and post-flight check list for each of these positions to make sure that no stone is left unturned at an event. I can safely say that my checklists have saved my company tens of thousands of dollars in the prevention of huge mistakes and it's easily made me more than $100,000 over the years in making sure my teams are properly prepared to maximize our sales.

If interested, you can visit my website and I have this as a product available for purchase: www.tophersbook.com/checklist

CHAPTER 30

ARE YOU COMMITTED OR PASSIONATE?

C ongratulations, you've made it through the entire book! If you have read this far, there is one thing I know about you: You are passionate about becoming the most successful professional speaker possible. What I'm uncertain of is whether or not you are committed.

In today's self-help culture, the line between passion and commitment has been erased and all too often people confuse the two. The world has never been filled with more highly motivated, passionate speakers who aren't doing anything significant with their careers. In order to succeed in any noble endeavor, you must move from the realm of passion into commitment. What is the difference?

A passionate person will get up early and stay up late. They will be the consummate optimist when things aren't going their way. They will constantly focus on their outcome and be patient, knowing that once they get a few more things in place, their good fortune will turn in their favor. While, on the surface, the passionate person seems to have it all together, they will forever struggle until they increase their level of commitment.

A committed person will get what needs to be done in the timeframe they set and not be willing to work 24/7 because they know that without a set timeframe or deadline, they will not stay focused on task. They will not use their current situation as an excuse for why they haven't achieved their future outcomes; instead, they spend their days changing their current situation to ensure their future outcome happens naturally. A committed person is willing to experience one major thing that passionate people will not: sacrifice. **A committed person will sacrifice their current level of comfort to ensure they are wildly comfortable in the end**. A committed person will sacrifice their safety and stability to go for it all, while the passionate person wants to live the life of their dreams immediately, not making the necessary sacrifice to achieve their long-term goals.

I have no doubt you are passionate about becoming a professional speaker. But are you committed to doing it? This chapter is dedicated to providing you with the necessary elements to succeed only if you are truly committed. Because the committed person will get excited at the challenges I'm about to lay out, but the passionate person will just come up with excuses and reasons for why they can't do these key things:

1. You must have a mentor—not a coach!

What is the difference? Well frankly, mostly the spelling, but here's my take on the two, and the differentiation is important. A coach may or may not have been more successful in the field they are coaching someone on. For example, most Olympic coaches were never gold medal Olympians. In fact, most of them never made it to the Olympics. They achieved a certain degree of success and the hit a plateau they could not surpass; however, this lack of success in their chosen endeavor does not mean they don't have the distinctions to be able to coach someone to even greater success than they achieved individually. Coaches are great, and they have an uncanny ability to see any situation that they are a coach in and know what needs to be adjusted to make powerful results.

In business, a good coach will rarely make recommendations or tell you what to do. Instead, they will ask you all the right questions to get you to make the correct conclusions yourself. This is a great technique and when a coach is skilled in this process, they can get you to make some amazing discoveries about yourself and your business.

A mentor, however, is someone who has achieved a level of success that you aspire to. Not only do they have the ability to see what necessary changes need to be made in your game plan like a coach, but they also speak from a greater level of authority because they have walked in your shoes already. This can often lead to faster results than coaching because a mentor has no problem taking the reins and telling you what to do. The results are much more immediate, but only if you have faith in the mentor and trust their judgment.

When Mr. Miyagi mentored Daniel in "The Karate Kid," he told him how to stain the fence, wax the cars, sand the floors, and paint the house. But he didn't tell him why. He just knew what needed to be done and he knew that in time, Daniel would see the genius behind his advice. Mr. Miyagi was a mentor, not a coach. You need to find a Mr. Miyagi.

2. Do what your mentor says!
Remember this phrase for the rest of your life:

Advice only works if you use it.

All too often, people get great advice from their friends, coaches, teachers, parents and mentors, but never do anything with it. If you ask for someone's advice and they take the time to give you a thoughtful recommendation, you owe it to yourself and the person who gave you the advice to actually go out and do something with it. Nothing will turn a mentor off faster than a protégé who does not do what they tell them to do. A true mentor will grow impatient and walk away from the relationship to find someone else who will materialize his or her advice into reality.

3. Make the sacrifice.

Here's why most people can't handle mentors: the advice they give is rarely easy to do. When you are given a set of instructions by a mentor, you can almost always guarantee they will not be simple tasks anyone could accomplish. It's okay; doing the hard things is what separates the winners from the losers. And in the world of business, there are such things as winners and losers. One thing that might help you to accept this notion of competition is to realize you can have competition in business without it being cutthroat. I think people often confuse the two. I have many people in the speaking business who are my competitors but we are not cutthroat in anyway and we get along well.

So remember this three-step approach to succeeding as a professional speaker:

1. Find a mentor
2. Do what your mentor says
3. Make the sacrifice

If you can incorporate all of the information in this book, congratulations—you are better person than I am. I started this book by admitting that I've made all the mistakes I mention in this book, I'll

end the book with a confession: **I still make some of these mistakes.**
It's been said that we teach what we need to learn the most. This book
is as much a guideline for me as I hope it will be for you. Don't try to
do it all at once. Take the pieces you know you can implement now and
get started. As your skillset grows, come back and incorporate more into
your profession.

If you are looking for a mentor in the professional speaking business,
I would love the opportunity to have a conversation with you about
such an endeavor. Please visit my website at www.tophermorrison.com
and see the various services I offer. If one of them speaks to you, just
reach out. I'm only a phone call away. Until we speak, take care, dare to
dream, and make each day an epic adventure!

ABOUT THE AUTHOR

Topher Morrison is the founder of Topher Communications Inc. A company based in Tampa FL that specializes in pitch development for business leaders. He is featured in the award-winning documentaries "The Compass" and "Riches," and his first book, *Stop Chasing Perfection & Settle for Excellence* has been hailed as 'The self-help book for people who are sick of self-help books.' His book, *Collaboration Economy*, co-authored with John Spencer Ellis, has become the go-to book for businesses preparing for the new Collaboration Age. In 2017 he was voted one of the Top 10 Business Speakers in Tampa Bay. Most recently, he was accepted onto the University of Tampa's Board of Fellows, and is a Professor of Practice in their entrepreneurship program.

His extensive speaking schedule, spanning over the past 25 years, has taken him throughout the US, UK, Australia, and Singapore and has earned him a global reputation as an expert in mass-communications and influence. Topher has spoken for top executives with American Express, Microsoft & Google, just to name a few.

In contrast to most professional speakers, Topher's shockingly honest, sometimes irreverent, and always down-to-earth approach is surprisingly infectious. His personality and straightforward manner are perfect for the businessperson who is tired of fleeting success in "self-help sinkholes." He is not afraid to tell it like it is and shatters the myth of achieving overnight success. Instead, Topher speaks to the person who could care less about motivational 'magic wands' and is more focused on getting tangible, proven strategies to become a key person of influence in their company, network, or industry.

In his personal life, he spends the majority of the time hanging out with his dog, Macie.

Morgan James
Speakers Group

www.TheMorganJamesSpeakersGroup.com

We connect Morgan James published
authors with live and online events
and audiences whom will benefit
from their expertise.